QUEENS

A CULINARY PASSPORT

QUEENS

A CULINARY PASSPORT

Exploring Ethnic Cuisine in
New York's Most Diverse Borough

Andrea Lynn

St. Martin's Griffin
New York

To Queens, which stole my heart 7 years ago
and has held on with a firm grip since

www.stmartins.com

Designed by Jonathan Bennett

Maps courtesy of jennasuedesign.com

The Library of Congress Cataloging-in-Publication Data is
available upon request.

ISBN 978-1-250-03987-3 (trade paperback)
ISBN 978-1-4668-5755-1 (e-book)

St. Martin's Griffin books may be purchased for educational,
business, or promotional use. For information on bulk
purchases, please contact Macmillan Corporate and Premium
Sales Department at 1-800-221-7945, extension 5442, or
write specialmarkets@macmillan.com.

First Edition: October 2014

10 9 8 7 6 5 4 3 2 1

CONTENTS

Introduction ix

Astoria 1
Athens Café 4
Taverna Kyclades 5
Kopiaste Taverna 11
Kabab Café 15
Gregory's 26 Corner Taverna 15
Food Shop: Titan Foods 19
King of Falafel and Shawarma 19
Astoria Walking Tour 22
Queens Food Pro: Meg Cotner 24

Long Island City 29
Food Shop: Slovack Czech Varieties 32
M. Wells Dinette 32
Sage General Store 35
Long Island City Walking Tour 41

Forest Hills/Rego Park 45
Ben's Best Kosher Deli 48
Eddie's Sweet Shop 53
Wafa's 58
Cheburechnaya 62
Forest Hills/Rego Park Walking Tour 64
Queens Food Pro: Famous Fat Dave 65

Corona 69
Tortilleria Nixtamel 72
Tortas Neza 77
Rincon Criollo 79
Tony's Pizzeria & Restaurant 85
Corona Walking Tour 88
Queens Food Pro: Myra Alperson 89

Sunnyside 93
Salt & Fat 97
Food Shop: Butcher Block 101
Romanian Garden 104
Natural Tofu Restaurant 106
Queens Food Pro: Max Falkowitz 110

Woodside 115
SriPraPhai 119
Tito Rad's Grill & Restaurant 124
Food Shop: Ottomanelli & Son's Prime Meat Shop . . 128
Food Shop: Phil-Am Foods 132
Queens Food Pro: Katrina Schultz Richter 133

Elmhurst 137
JoJu Modern Vietnamese Sandwiches 140
Ayada Thai 143
Food Shop: U.S. Supermarket 144
La Esquinita del Camaron Mexicano 145
Elmhurst Mex Grocery Company 148
Elmhust Walking Tour 149
Queens Food Pro: Lesley Tellez 151

Jackson Heights 153
Himalayan Yak 156
Pio Pio 161
Kababish 164
Little Tibet 165
Food Shop: Patel Brothers 170
Jackson Heights Walking Tour 172
Queens Food Pro: Jeff Orlick 173

Flushing 177
Hunan Kitchen of Grand Sichuan 180
Golden Shopping Mall 183
Food Shop: Assi Plaza 186
Food Shop: Chung Fat Supermarket 188
Maxin Bakery 188
Jade Asian Restaurant 191
Fang Gourmet Tea 193
Soy Bean Chen Flower Shop 195
Fu Run 197
Flushing Walking Tour 200
Queens Food Pro: Joe DiStefano 202

Acknowledgments 205
Index 207

INTRODUCTION

Queens had my back from my first day as a borough resident. Juggling moving boxes as I shuttled my stuff to my apartment in Astoria, my typical klutziness sent a pile of belongings crashing to the ground with a mess of clothes and books sprawled all over the sidewalk. In Manhattan, I would have been left scrambling as commuters and tourists trampled their way across my stuff. So I was shocked that a number of people stopped what they were doing to rush over and help me. I knew then that Queens was different.

Every time I hear friends talk about moving to Brooklyn, I'll pipe up, "Well, what about Queens?" They'll roll their eyes at me and continue with their discussion. Queens remains the step-sister to the more glamorous Manhattan and trendier Brooklyn, a bronze medal borough to many but a winner to those who know its worth. Perhaps what sets Queens apart is what made me fall in love with it: the friendliness of strangers, mom-and-pop stores, pockets of ethnic diversity, and more. With this book, I want to share and inspire a little Queens love.

Queens is a massive borough, so not every distinctive restaurant or food shop can be profiled in the span of a 200-page culinary guidebook. In no way is this book meant to be all-inclusive, but rather a series of snapshots of the borough's offerings. I've chosen what I think is a good representation of the borough for those who want just a taste of it. It's also a subway friendly book, concentrating on the parts of the borough accessible via our city's inter-borough transit system—sorry, Rockaway Beach, maybe next time!

For more regular Queens-centered food content, refer to the offers of Edible Queens or the Web sites *Serious Eats*, *We Heart Astoria*, *Jeff Tastes*, and *Chopsticks and Marrow*. Here's to the start of a Queens love affair.

Indonesia Bazaar held in the parking lot at Masjid Al-Hikmah Mosque in Astoria on random dates during warm weather and deemed some of the best Indonesian food in NYC by Serious Eats Max Falkowtiz. *(photo by Andrea Lynn)*

RUJAK CINGUR
→ GUDEG KOMPLIT
→ AYAM BAKAR
→ SATE PADANG
→ EMPEK Z
→ GULE
→ BAKSO
→ BALADO DAGING

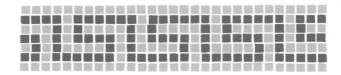

Astoria

One of the zippiest subway rides from Manhattan, Astoria is probably the first neighborhood in Queens a Manhattan resident might get a taste of, an experience that usually takes place in a beer garden. But Astoria's cultural beauty is far deeper and more complex than what you might find in a beer garden. When I first moved to Astoria, I held a special fondness for the European feel of the neighborhood. In nice weather, the outdoor tables at **Athens Café** are crammed with Greeks and non-Greeks sipping frappés. In the summer, elderly Italian ladies dig through the sale rack of the fruit and vegetable stands across the street looking for less-than-perfect tomatoes for their sauces. The checkered outdoor tablecloths and straight-from-Greece carafes usher in a Mediterranean feel at **Gregory's 26 Corner Taverna**. While slowly devouring the restaurant's divine octopus appetizer one day, I chatted with two girls who were visiting New York City (and Astoria) just because they had heard it would be so similar to the tavernas they had frequented in Greece. And it was, they swooned, as they ate gyros and sipped the strong Greek coffee.

But Greek isn't the only ethnicity represented in Astoria. A stretch of Steinway Street is referred to as "Little Egypt" due to the North African concentration. Astoria's Little Egypt is highlighted by **Kabab Café**, opened by chef Ali El Sayed in 1987, whom Anthony Bourdain described as "a legend among hard-core foodies; reason alone to go to Queens." The area is also home to many Italians, who flock there for homemade mozzarella, homemade sausage, and imported Italian goods at **Sorriso Italian Pork Store** and Italian sweets from **Gian Piero Bakery** across the street.

Athens Café

Greek Frappé
Yield: 1 serving

(photo by Janis Turk)

Hailed as the national coffee of Greece, the frappé is a frothy concoction of coffee granulates and water, made foamy thanks to a frappé machine. The drink can't exactly be replicated without the machine, but you can come close by putting the drink into a container and shaking it, a lot! The Greek Nescafé Taster's Choice is stronger than its American counterpart. If you can find it, Athens Café suggests using South African Nescafé, which also has a more robust feel. Instead, I just use more of the easier-found American version. If you find yourself verging on a frappé addiction like I do, machines can be bought at the Greek mecca, Titan Foods. Recipe adapted from Athens Café.

1 tablespoon Nescafé Taster's Choice Instant Coffee
½ cup water
Sugar (optional)
3 to 4 ice cubes
Milk or heavy cream, if desired

In a 2-cup or 4-cup container with lid, add coffee, water, sugar (optional), and ice cubes. (I've found a 2-cup Mason jar ideal for making these.) Tighten lid, and shake, shake, shake until the ice cubes are mostly dissolved. Pour into an 8-ounce glass, and serve. Note that the larger the container you use to shake, the more foam you will have.

ATHENS CAFÉ
Info: 32-07 30th Ave., Astoria; 718-626-2164; athenscafeny.com
See You There: Take the N or Q train to the 30th Ave. stop

(photo by Janis Turk)

Taverna Kyclades

A quick way to begin an argument between Astorians is by asking them to choose their favorite Greek restaurant, a difficult task since Astoria is the Greek food capital of New York. With so many Greek restaurants to choose from, when I'm forced to pick between neighborhood faves like Agnanti and Stamatis, just to name a few, I'll profess to being a Kyclades gal.

The restaurant name is derived from the "Cyclades," a group of Greek islands south of the mainland. With its turquoise interior and seafood-heavy menu, this restaurant has an authentic Greek vibe. Restaurant patron Larry Finkelstein said it best when he labeled Kyclades as "the BMW of restaurants" due to the huge portion sizes, the fact the restaurant runs like a well-oiled machine, and the owner's magnificent character in customer interactions.

Owner Ardian Skenderi thinks the key to the restaurant's popularity is its consistency. "Well, this is quality food, and the portions are big enough. Every time you come, it's the same. You come here six months later, and we always keep it the same. People like that and appreciate it." The portion sizes are indeed huge and, in fact, Kyclades is one of the best examples I can use to illustrate the superiority of Queens portions to Manhattan portions. (Expect lots of leftovers!)

Popular menu items, according to Ardian, are the grilled octopus, calamari (grilled or fried), and the ever-requested Greek salad, which is also one of Ardian's steadfast daily eats, along with chicken kebabs, and something from the ocean, like fresh sea bass or scallops. And who can argue with the healthy appeal of the Mediterranean diet? Ardian thinks it adds to the restaurant's popularity.

Another not-so-secret slice of their success is high-quality ingredients that aren't barraged with non-necessities—jumbo shrimp or whole fish like branzino are grilled and drizzled with nothing more than Greek olive oil, dried oregano, and sea salt. "You have to make sure the fish is fresh all the time. That's why I go to the market myself," he says. Ardian also believes in another fundamental to the success of the restaurant, which I think is a good motto for life (as well as the restaurant business). "I love what I do," he says. "Basically you don't have to know too many things. If you know how to do two or three things, and you do them correctly, you'll be successful."

TAVERNA KYCLADES
Info: 33-07 Ditmars Blvd., Astoria; 718-545-8666; tavernakyclades.com

See You There: Take the N to Queens to the last stop, Ditmars.

For an Authentic Experience: Ardian recommends a Greek Salad, Grilled Octopus, and the Pan-Fried Greek Cheese for appetizers, finishing with whole fish as the main course. Don't bother asking what the fresh fish of the day is because if it's in stock that day, it's fresh.

Greek salad appetizer at Taverna Kyclades. (photo by Janis Turk)

Greek Salad

Yield: 4 servings

"You've got to understand how to work with the salad," advises Kyclades owner Ardian Skenderi. "When you make a Greek salad you start with the lettuce, red onions, and tomato, so the color is right there." But don't get the wrong idea—the iceberg lettuce is only a small component of the salad rather than the overriding ingredient. Also, the restaurant uses feta straight from Greece. Ardian says the organic grazing of the sheep make for a better cheese product, and that it's best to buy feta cheese wedges instead of the crumbled varieties. "When the cheese is crushed up, you don't know how good it is," he says. This recipe is adapted from Ardian Skenderi's.

2 cups chopped iceberg lettuce
2 large cucumbers, peeled and chopped into bite-size pieces
4 medium tomatoes, sliced
½ cup pitted Kalamata olives
¼ small red onion, sliced
8 to 10 pepperoncini peppers
½ teaspoon dried oregano
¼ teaspoon kosher salt
⅛ teaspoon freshly ground black pepper
2 tablespoons red wine vinegar
5 tablespoons extra-virgin olive oil
2 (¼-pound) wedges feta cheese

In a large bowl, add lettuce. Then, top with a mixture of tomatoes and cucumbers. Decorate with olives, red onion slices, and peppers. In a small bowl, add ¼ teaspoon oregano, salt, pepper, and vinegar. Using a fork, whisk together ingredients as you pour the oil into the dressing to emulsify. Pour dressing over salad. Top with feta wedges, and sprinkle with remaining ¼ teaspoon oregano.

Broiled Whole Fish with Oregano and Lemon

Yield: 4 servings

Enter my new favorite way of cooking fish, thanks to this recipe from Taverna Kyclades: Just slap it on a baking sheet with spices and lemon, place it under the broiler, and dinner is ready in mere minutes. Ardian stresses that the key is buying good-quality fish. He can walk into a fish market and tell what is fresh, simply by looking at it. For less experienced fish buyers, he recommends asking to touch the fish: If it's fresh, it will be firm. If it's not, it will be mushy and your finger will sink when touching it. The whole branzino is the most popular fish request at Kyclades, but any whole fish of the specified size (1½ pounds) will do. For this recipe, one fish feeds two people. Recipe adapted from Ardian Skenderi.

1 teaspoon kosher salt
½ teaspoon freshly ground black pepper
2 teaspoons dried oregano
2 (1½-pound) whole fish (like branzino, red snapper, or trout),
    cleaned, scaled, rinsed, and dried with paper towels
Olive oil, as needed
6 garlic cloves
2 lemons, sliced

Broiled Whole Fish with Oregano and Lemon.
(photo by Janis Turk)

Preheat the broiler. In a small bowl, combine salt, pepper, and oregano.

Prepare a baking sheet by lining it with foil, and then coating it with cooking spray. Place both fish on the baking sheet, positioning the fish so the head is to your left and the cavity opening is facing you. On the top of the fish, make 3 to 4 diagonal slices down the length of the fish, about ½- to 1-inch deep, and about 1½ inches apart. Generously drizzle oil inside the fish cavities and on the top of the fish. Then, divide each oregano-salt mixture between both fish, sprinkling it inside the cavity and on top of the fish again. Stuff each cavity with 3 garlic cloves and as many lemon slices as will fit. Reserve remaining lemon to serve with fish.

Place the fish under the broiler, and cook 3 minutes. Turn the baking sheet 180 degrees, and continue to cook until skin is browned and fish flesh can be flaked with a fork, about 3 to 4 more minutes. Remove from oven, use a spatula to transfer fish to a plate, and serve with the Greek Lemon Roasted Potatoes.

Substitution Can't find whole fish? Just substitute with another Kyclades favorite: jumbo shrimp. Sprinkle 1½ pounds of cleaned, butterflied jumbo shrimp with salt, pepper, oregano, and olive oil. Place on a foil-lined and greased baking sheet and broil for about 2 to 3 minutes per side.

Greek Lemon Roasted Potatoes
Yield: 4 servings

With a lemony flavor that walks the line of almost being too tart, creating these potatoes became an obsession of mine when I first moved to Astoria. I marinated, roasted, and boiled the potatoes in a hefty amount of lemon juice, never happy with the subpar results. So when I started this Queens cookbook, I knew I had to delve into the secret of the lemon potatoes. In talking to a few Greek restaurants, a couple common denominators became apparent. The first is that the potatoes must cook in an even layer of the lemon juice mixture, almost braising in the liquid.

Overcrowding ruins the results because the potatoes can't soak up the lemony goodness, which I realized had been one of my fatal flaws. The second factor was that everyone agreed chicken concentrate (vegetarian or not) is a must, although I couldn't ever get a reason why. This recipe, based on the Taverna Kyclades' recipe for lemon potatoes, is to be served with the Broiled Whole Fish with Oregano and Lemon. For intensely lemony potatoes, use the high end of the recommended lemon juice amount—¾ cup (which is my preference); for a less lemony flavor, go for the lower end of ½ cup. Sometimes I crank the oven to 450°F during the last 15 minutes to ensure extra-browned potatoes. Recipe adapted from Ardian Skenderi.

4 large Russet potatoes (about 2 pounds) or 8 medium
  Russet potatoes
¼ cup extra-virgin olive oil
1 teaspoon dried oregano, plus more for garnish
½ teaspoon kosher salt
¼ teaspoon freshly ground pepper
½ cup boiling water
1 chicken bouillon cube*
½ to ¾ cup fresh lemon juice (about 4 to 6 lemons)

Preheat oven to 400°F. Peel the potatoes, then, cut each potato in half lengthwise, then cut each half into quarters. (If you're using medium potatoes, just peel and quarter each potato.) Add potatoes to a large Pyrex or roasting pan, making sure the potatoes are in a single layer. (If they won't fit into one layer, divide potatoes and liquid between 2 pans. They won't cook properly if not in an even layer.) Sprinkle the potatoes with oil, oregano, salt, and pepper. Using tongs or your hands, toss potatoes to coat with oil and spices.

In a small bowl, add water and bouillon cube, whisking with a fork until the cube dissolves. Pour over the potatoes, along with the lemon juice. Tightly cover the pan with foil, and roast in the oven for 30 minutes. If the lemon juice mixture is evaporating too fast, add ¼-cup increments of water during the cooking process. Remove the foil, and continue cooking until potatoes are browned and fork-tender, about another 30 to 45 minutes. Remove from the oven, garnish with additional oregano if desired, and serve with a spoon (the better to get the lemony sauce with the potatoes).

* **Substitution** ½ cup chicken stock = ½ cup boiling water + bouillon cube.

Kopiaste Taverna

Kopiaste reflects another Mediterranean cuisine, Cypriot, which has almost as many similarities as differences in relation to Greek food. An island in the Mediterranean Sea, Cyprus is famous for food with a high concentration in pork, coriander, cumin, and parsley. Kopiaste began getting an onslaught of customers after reviews in the *Wall Street Journal* and *Village Voice* touted their Cyprus mezze, a food tour through the country through mini shared plates for the steal of $22. "Ninety-five percent of people eat the mezze," says owner George Georgiou. "They say it's amazing. They take it home because it's so much food they cannot finish it." (Notice the pattern of left-overs in Queens restaurants?)

Another popular Cyprus specialty available at the restaurant is the sheftalia, homemade Cypriot sausage made from ground pork, parsley, and onions rolled in caul fat. "It's delicious," says George. "It's very unique and very popular in Cyprus. We sell hundreds of these. People come and they say, 'Give me one hundred for a party.'" Kopiaste isn't trying to compete with the Greek establishments in the area—and, in fact, the owner helmed a popular Astoria Greek restaurant in the early eighties—but rather spread a little foodie knowledge about Cypriot cuisine. And that he does through the mezze offerings like Taramasalata (an airy version of fish roe spread), Koupepia (the Cypriot way of stuffing grape leaves, pork included, of course), Keftedes (pork meatballs), and more.

KOPIASTE TAVERNA
Info: 23-15 31st St., Astoria; 718-932-3220

See You There: Take the N train to Queens to the last stop, Ditmars. The restaurant is between 23rd Ave. and 23rd Rd.

For an Authentic Experience: There's a reason why a majority of the clientele order the Cyprus mezze—because it's a culinary walk though Cyprus. However, if going the entrée route, George recommends the Stifado Kouneli, a rabbit and onion stew braised in vinegar, for a taste of a Cypriot meal.

Red Wine Pork (Afelia) with Cracked Wheat Pilaf (Pourgouri)

Yield: 4 servings

Both the Afelia and Pourgouri can be served as mezze options in Cyprus or as a main meal, as done in this version. The red wine—braised pork came out slightly more red-tinted than the restaurant's version, so be prepared. There's something unglamorous yet comforting about this recipe—it seems outwardly plain, but when I eat it or make it for company, it's completely devoured.

Kopiaste cook Paraskevi Roussopoulos, from whom the recipe is adapted, says the key to the cracked wheat pilaf is to cook the vermicelli until it's golden brown, so it isn't the same color as the bulgur wheat. The restaurant makes the pilaf completely off-heat, letting it steam for 90 minutes; but I sped up the process.

FOR THE RED WINE PORK:
2 pounds lean pork shoulder, trimmed of fat and cut into
  small pieces
1 ½ tablespoons coriander seed
1 tablespoon ground coriander
1 cup red wine, divided
1 ½ tablespoons olive oil
½ teaspoon kosher salt
¼ teaspoon freshly ground black pepper
chicken stock (optional)

FOR THE CRACKED WHEAT PILAF:
1 ½ tablespoons olive oil
1 medium yellow onion, chopped
1 cup broken pieces angel hair pasta or capellini
3 cups chicken stock
1 tablespoon tomato paste
1 large tomato, chopped
¼ teaspoon kosher salt
1 cup coarse bulgur wheat

Marinate the pork: In a bowl or ziplock bag, add pork, coriander seeds, ground coriander, and ½ cup red wine. Marinate meat mixture at least 1 hour.

Make the pork: In a Dutch oven, warm olive oil over medium-high heat. Add pork and marinade to the pan, along with remaining ½ cup red wine, salt, and pepper. Bring liquid to a boil. Then, cover with lid and reduce heat to low. Cook until meat is tender, about 1½ hours, checking occasionally to make sure there is enough liquid (adding chicken stock if needed).

Make the pilaf: In a heavy-duty medium pot, warm ½ table-spoon oil over medium-high heat and add onion. Sauté, stirring occasionally, until onions are soft, about 5 minutes. Add remaining 1 tablespoon oil, and angel hair pasta. Stirring constantly, let the pasta brown, about 2 to 4 minutes. Once browned, immediately add chicken stock, tomato paste, tomato, and salt. Stir to combine and add bulgur wheat. Cover with lid, and let mixture simmer 5 minutes. Remove from heat, and let pilaf sit 5 to 10 minutes. Serve pilaf with pork.

Red Wine Pork (Afelia) and Cracked Wheat Pilaf (Pourgouri) at Kopiaste Taverna. *(photo by Janis Turk)*

Cypriot Pork Sausage (Sheftalia)

Yield: around 20 sausages

This was my first experience working with the natural spider web of caul fat—available at most butchers—which is the membrane around the intestines. And, much to my surprise, I fell a little in love with it. It's an easier way of making sausages than putting them through the double rotation of a meat grinder and then squeezing into natural casings. The Sheftalia is also supremely flavorful for having only a handful of ingredients. Grilling works best for cooking the caul fat–wrapped sausages, followed by broiling and then sautéing or oven-roasting. A majority of the caul fat melts during the cooking process, leaving the meat in the molded shape. Recipe adapted from Kopiaste cook Paraskevi Roussopoulos.

    1½ pounds high-quality ground pork
    1 large white onion, finely chopped
    1 bunch fresh flat-leaf parsley, finely chopped
    ½ teaspoon kosher salt
    ½ teaspoon freshly ground black pepper
    ½ pound caul fat, washed and soaked in water for at least
       10 minutes

In a large bowl, add ground pork, onion, parsley, salt, and pepper. Use a spoon or clean hands to thoroughly mix ingredients together.

Take a piece of caul fat and lay it on a cutting board. Place a rounded mound of the meat mixture (about 1 heaping tablespoon) into a corner of the caul fat. Roll meat in caul fat until completely covered, about 1½ to 2 times. Use kitchen shears or a knife to cut the rolled Sheftalia from the remaining caul fat. Repeat until all the meat is wrapped.

To grill, cook the Sheftalia on a hot grill until fully cooked, about 12 to 15 minutes, turning occasionally to brown all sides. If you don't have a grill, just cook in the broiler (see headnote) or sauté to brown all sides of the sausage in a large ovenproof pan and then cook in a 400°F oven until inside is fully cooked, about 5 to 7 minutes.

Kabab Café

Part of the charm of this Egyptian enclave is owner/chef Ali El Sayed. Situated on the tiny stretch of Steinway Street known as "Little Cairo," Kabab Café is a few buildings down from Mombar restaurant, owned by El Sayed's brother, Moustafa. (Check out Moustafa's own artwork swirled on his building as you walk by.) Ali has been described as being close to a culinary god from ethnic food heavyweights such as Anthony Bourdain and Andrew Zimmern. There's no handheld menu, just Ali lovingly dictating that day's menu availability. Start with the sumac-dusted mezze platter and pick from the day's choices, usually on the culinary wild side, like sweetbreads, lamb cheeks, and kidneys. Bring cash; rumor has it that inquiring about prices won't get you into Ali's good graces. Two of the primary pluses about the restaurant can also swing negative: 1) Unpredictable is the mantra, as patrons never know what unique Middle Eastern delicacies will be showcased on their plates. I've also watched lunch-goers wait for Ali to arrive for the lunch shift only to give up and leave when he doesn't show. 2) Ali's large personality fills the cozy restaurant space, and he never shoos diners out the door. Yet if you're shivering in the cold waiting two hours for a table, there's a bit of a wish for a quicker table turnover. Ali's Kabab Café is an experience you won't forget; just be armed with a backup restaurant in case you can't get a table, and lots of cash in case you can.

KABAB CAFÉ
Info: 2512 Steinway St.; 718-728-9858

See You There: About a 10-minute walk north from the 30th Avenue stop off the N/Q train on Steinway.

Gregory's 26 Corner Taverna

While the other Greek restaurants in Astoria channel Greek vibes, Gregory's 26 Corner actually feels like you've been instantly transported to Greece. At least half the tables are occupied by Greek speakers with the hum of Greek television adding more chatter to the small restaurant. There's even Greek beer and wine served in carafes straight from the motherland.

Who orders what at this restaurant is entirely based on ethnicity, according to Frideriki Bletsas, who cheerfully cooks and serves up Greek fare daily and owns the restaurant with her husband, Gregory. Americans order the smelts, octopus, fried peppers, and the specials. Greeks prefer heartier fare like moussaka or roasted leg of lamb. Sporting a heavy Greek accent despite more than forty-five years living in the United States, Frideriki admits her octopus has become somewhat legendary for the restaurant. "People go to other places to try their octopus and then come back to compare it to mine. None are as good as mine," she says. And I have to admit that she's right.

GREGORY'S 26 CORNER TAVERNA
Info: 26-02 23rd Ave., Astoria; 718-777-5511

See You There: Take the N train to Queens to the last stop, Ditmars. Walk south on 23rd Ave. about 10 minutes, past other restaurants into a mostly residential area. You'll worry that you're lost, but don't worry—you're not!

For an Authentic Experience: The octopus is a must. Other recommendations include fried meatballs, zucchini patties, peppers stuffed with feta cheese, the fried smelts, and any of the fresh fish.

Grilled or Broiled Octopus
Yield: 4 appetizer servings

This is an appetizer at Gregory's; to bulk it up into a meal, double the recipe and add an order of oven-roasted beets or sautéed dandelion greens, two sides served at the restaurant. Recipe adapted from Frideriki Bletsas.

1 (4- to 5-pound) octopus, cleaned
4 to 5 garlic cloves
2 teaspoons dried oregano
1 lemon, halved
3½ tablespoons extra-virgin olive oil
2 large tomatoes, sliced
2 large cucumbers, peeled (optional) and sliced
½ tablespoon red wine vinegar, as needed
Kosher salt and freshly ground black pepper, as needed

The Grilled Octopus appetizer
at Gregory's 26 Corner Taverna.
(photo by Janis Turk)

Using either a knife or kitchen shears, remove each tentacle from the octopus head. Discard the head, and cut the tentacles into a few pieces. Add octopus to a large Dutch oven or a heavy-duty large pot, and cover with water and salt. Bring to a boil over high heat. Cover, and reduce to medium-low to low heat so liquid is simmering. Let octopus cook for 2 to 3 hours until very tender. (To check, I recommend removing an octopus tentacle and cutting it with a knife to see if it's tender.) Remove octopus tentacles from liquid, transfer to a container, and drizzle 2 tablespoons olive oil over it. Refrigerate until ready to serve.

When ready to serve, in a large bowl, add tomatoes, cucumbers, and red onion. Drizzle with vinegar, remaining 1½ tablespoons olive oil, salt, and pepper, tossing to combine. Cut octopus tentacles into pieces. Grill until slightly charred, just a few minutes per side. If you don't have a grill, don't worry. Warm a large nonstick sauté pan over high heat with ½ tablespoon olive oil and sauté until octopus is warmed and slightly charred, a few minutes per side. Divide salad between the plates and top with octopus. Serve.

Spicy Greek Cheese Dip (Tirokafteri) ■■■■■■■■
Yield: 4 appetizer servings ■■■■■■■■■■■■■■

I like to think of this Greek Cheese Dip as a Greek form of pimento cheese, but with feta and olive oil in place of the Southern mainstays of cheddar and mayo. For a quicker version of this cheese dip, use 2 roasted red bell peppers and 1 to 2 raw jalapeños. Recipe adapted from Frideriki Bletsas.

    1 medium green bell pepper
    1 to 2 jalapeño peppers
    8 ounces Greek feta cheese
    Ground cayenne powder, to taste
    2 to 3 tablespoons extra-virgin olive oil
    Warmed pitas, to serve

Either on a grill, a gas stovetop, or in a broiler, roast all peppers, rotating constantly, until blackened on each side, up to 10 minutes. Transfer peppers to a bowl, cover with plastic wrap, and let sit 15 minutes. When cool, remove charred skin from pepper using your fingers. Remove seeds from each pepper. Chop peppers into very small pieces or use a food processor to finely chop.

In a bowl, add chopped peppers, feta cheese, and cayenne pepper to taste. Work mixture constantly with your hands until a paste is formed. Add cayenne powder to taste. To serve, drizzle with olive oil and eat with pita bread. Enjoy with wine (instructions straight from Frideriki).

FOOD SHOP: Titan Foods

Boasting the largest retail Greek specialty store in the United States, Titan (pronounced Tee-tan, not Tie-tan) Foods is a Greek wonderland. Ardian Skenderi of Taverna Kyclades shops here for sea salt (his salt of choice), olives, pepperoncini, olive oil, lima beans, and pita bread while Gregory from 26 Corner Taverna relies on the store for vegetables and lamb. According to the manager, the store's bestsellers are Arahova feta cheese, Kalamata extra-virgin olive oil, and Tsoureki bread, a sweet yeast-based bread normally found only during Greek Easter but so popular that it's available year-round at Titan. Their homemade spinach pie, a thick layer of dill-scented spinach and feta between flaky phyllo dough, is also a top seller. And be sure to check out the vast array of feta cheeses, the olive display, and the wall of pitas. There's also cooked octopus ready for the taking at the deli counter.

Info: 25-56 31st St., Astoria; 718-626-7771; titanfoods.net

See You There: Take the N or Q train to the 30th Ave. stop. Walk north on 31st St.

King of Falafel and Shawarma

I'm a carnivore through and through. So the fact that I'll pass up meat in favor of falafel from Freddy Zeidaies (he is the king of falafel, after all) is a true testament to how good it is. He says it's the oval shape, versus a round ball, that is the key to his magical falafel: The outside gets crispy while keeping the inside moist. The two-time Vendy Award winner serves the falafel on a platter or rolled into a pita. (My advice is to go for the platter; I'm a sucker for über-crispy falafel, and I think it gets soggier quicker when rolled into the pita.) He also uses it to take the pain out cart-side of waiting, feeding people in line piping hot falafel straight from the fryer basket. And if that doesn't tempt you enough, the meat platters like the Shawarma (beef and lamb), Omar Plate (chicken and shawarma), and Freddy's Junior (kefta and chicken) are bursting with flavor even before they are smothered in tahini, a magical white sauce, and (optional) hot sauce.

KING OF FALAFEL AND SHAWARMA
Info: 30th Street and Broadway, Astoria; 718-838-8029; thekingfalafel.com

See You There: right off the Broadway stop of the N/Q train, or the newest location at 33rd Street and 30th Avenue, off the 30th Avenue stop of the N/Q train.

King of Falafel's Famous Falafel

Yield: 6 servings

While the recipe instructs soaking the beans overnight, I found the quick-soaking method to work just as well: Add beans and 4 cups of water to a pot; bring to a boil over high heat and cook just 1 minute. Cover and let soak for at least 1 hour. Recipe adapted from Freddy Zeidaies.

1 (16-ounce) bag dried chickpeas
1 medium onion, quartered
3 cloves garlic
½ cup chopped parsley
½ red bell pepper
2 teaspoons turmeric
2 teaspoons paprika
1 teaspoon cardamom
1 teaspoon nutmeg
1 teaspoon cinnamon
1½ teaspoons kosher salt
¾ teaspoon freshly ground black pepper
2 teaspoons ground cumin
2 teaspoons ground coriander
1 teaspoon red hot pepper flakes
3 teaspoons baking powder
¾ cup water
Vegetable oil, as needed for deep frying
Pitas, lettuce, tomato, and tahini, to serve

Falafel mixture being scooped and formed at King of Falafel & Shawarma. (photo by Janis Turk)

Pick out foreign matter from between the chickpeas. Place in a large bowl and cover generously with water. Soak overnight.

The next day, drain the chickpeas in a colander. Place in a large bowl, and add onion, garlic, parsley, and bell pepper. Run through the fine blade of a meat grinder or purée in a food processor. Add spices, 2 teaspoons baking powder, and ¼ cup water. Mix well.

In a small dish, mix the remaining 1 teaspoon baking powder and ½ cup water. Use the liquid to moisten the palm of your hands and form balls ⅓ cup size with the chickpea mixture. Flatten them a little to make into an oval shape. Use a deep fryer or fill a heavy-bottom pot with canola oil. Deep fry them in oil at medium-high heat until golden brown, about 3 to 4 minutes. Using a slotted spoon, remove falafel from hot oil onto a paper towel-lined plate. Season with salt. Serve piping hot in halved loaves of pita, topped with lettuce, tomato, and tahini sauce.

Homemade sausages at Sorriso's Italian Pork Store. *(photo by Janis Turk)*

Astoria Walking Tour

Take the R subway train into Queens and exit at the Steinway Street stop. Make a right on Broadway, and walk one block to Ⓐ **The Queens Kickshaw** (40-17 Broadway Ave.; 718-777-0913), which specializes in fancy grilled cheese (hello, kimchee-stuffed grilled cheese), specialty coffee, craft beers, and a vast array of ciders. Try the Gouda grilled cheese, made with black bean hummus, guava jam, and pickled jalapeños. Next, walk back to Steinway, make a right, and walk 1½ (long) blocks to Ⓑ **Rizzo's Fine Pizza** (30-13 Steinway St.; 718-721-9862) for a slice of their famous square pizza they've been making since 1959. Each thin, crisp Sicilian slice is covered in robust sauce and topped with a modest slice of creamy mozzarella and a sprinkle of Parmesan. Continue up the block to 30th Avenue, make a right, and walk one block to Ⓒ **Cedars Meat House** (41-08 30th Ave.; 718-606-1244) and take your pick from oh-so-garlicky Lebanese sandwiches filled with meats and the likes of fried cauliflower, fried eggplant, or falafel. Don't forget to peek at the grocery selection in the back. Continue north on 30th Avenue to the family-owned Italian wonderland that is Ⓓ **Sorriso Italian Pork Store** (44-16 30th Ave.; 718-728-4392). Asking for samples is welcomed and the owner and his son will happily dole out the homemade sausages (in varieties like orange-fennel and olive) and house-made mozzarella cheese. Tuck into an eggplant Parmesan sandwich or take a jar of their fantastically flavorful jarred meat sauce. Make sure to ask if they have any fat left over from the prosciutto; freeze to cut into chunks and render for your next batch of marinara in a little trick they taught me. Across the street, swing by  **Gian Piero Bakery** (44-17 30th Ave.; 718-274-8959) for rainbow cookies, some of the best cannolis to grace Astoria, and my particular favorite, the very potent Baba Rum, a spongy dessert soaked in liqueur. Backtrack south to take a leisurely walk down 30th Avenue, loading up on the Cypriot sausage, sheftalia, or other meats at **International Meat Market** (36-12 30th Ave.; 718-626-6656) and then have a drink at **Sweet Afton** (30-09 34th St.; 718-777-2570), an inviting candlelit bar with creative cocktails, a thoughtful selection of beers on tap, and a small menu of quality food, including a killer burger and a bacon mac and cheese. Continue a few more blocks to the subway and take the N or Q back to Manhattan. If you can continue the gluttony, walk one avenue south to 31st Ave. to visit **Café Boulis** (31-15 31st Ave.; 718-806-1014) for pillows of Greek fried dough goodness. When asked, you'll want it the "Greek way," coated in honey, cinnamon, and powdered sugar.

QUEENS FOOD PRO: Meg Cotner, author of *Food Lovers' Guide to Queens*

What made you move to Queens and how long have you lived here? I moved to Queens because I couldn't afford rents in Brooklyn, which was my first choice. I moved here August 2005; I've been here for eight years always in the [Astoria] Ditmars neighborhood.

What's your Queens claim to food fame? I have been writing about the food in Queens since 2006. I've written online at About.com, Real Cheap Eats, and We Heart Astoria, and in print for the *New York Daily News*, *Specialty Food Magazine*, *BORO Magazine*, and I am the author of *Food Lovers' Guide to Queens*, a guidebook to restaurants, markets, and specialty food shops in the borough.

What's the most surprising experience (foodwise) you've had in Queens? My first taste of octopus was at Taverna Kyclades in Astoria. It was grilled and served with a little olive oil. I expected it to be like calamari—kind of rubbery. But it was not that way at all! I loved how tender and meaty it was. I'm an octopus convert.

Any favorite Queens memories? I love the Epitaphios, which is the procession on Orthodox Good Friday—it moves from St. Irene Monastery to St. Markella Orthodox Church. I think it's one of the really special things about living in Astoria. I also remember the first time I laid eyes on Astoria Park and the Hell Gate Bridge, and I was blown away by how beautiful it was.

Describe your ideal eating day in Queens: Breakfast would be the huevos rancheros and a pineapple agua fresca at The Haab in Sunnyside; the Gouda sandwich and an iced matcha tea at The Queens Kickshaw for lunch; cocktails at Via Trenta before dinner; and spicy avocado and goat cheese crostini, marinated carrot and feta salad, and Rain wine at Il Bambino for dinner. Dessert would be the Baby Jesus Cake at Vesta.

Is there a string of restaurants that you constantly recommend to others? I recommend Il Bambino in Astoria; Woodside Café in Woodside/Jackson Heights; Golden Palace in Flushing; Zum Stammtisch in Glendale; Krystal's in Woodside; Danny Brown Wine Bar in Forest Hills.

What are a few under-the-radar food places in Queens? Duzan in Astoria, Gregory's 26 Corner Taverna in Astoria, Slovak Czech Varieties in LIC, The Haab in Sunnyside, Thailand's Center Point in Woodside, Apollo Bakery in Flushing. The baked goods at Engeline's in Woodside.

Any Queens restaurant, food shop, truck, etc. that closed down for which you're still in mourning? I still lament the closing of Mundo in Astoria.

Any specific dishes from Queens restaurants that you've always wanted to make at home? I would love to learn to make phyllo dough at home so I can make Greek pies and baklava (a current obsession) truly from scratch. I'd also like to learn how to make hand-shaved Henanese noodles. Vesta's Baby Jesus Cake. Peruvian Chicha Morada from Urubamba in Jackson Heights. Hazelnut cannoli at Lulu's Italian-American bakery in Floral Park.

What is your favorite...

Italian restaurant in Queens: Vesta, for the modern take on Italian food and the use of local ingredients.

Thai restaurant in Queens: SriPraPhai, for their expansive menu and my favorite penang curry in town. The crispy watercress salad is also fabulous. Something about that dressing and the texture of the fried watercress is epic.

Chinese restaurant in Queens: Golden Palace for the delicious Dongbei cuisine.

Pizza in Queens: This is a very hard question, but I am perpetually in love with the bakery slices at Rose & Joe's. The sauce is so good—tangy yet sweet, and the dough is wonderful. They use regular mozzarella, too, nothing out of the ordinary. The combination is spectacular. I could eat it every day.

Greek in Queens: Gregory's 26 Corner Taverna for their fresh Greek food, great octopus, and excellent dips.

Mexican in Queens: Tacos Morelos in Jackson Heights for the tlacoyos, and the queso taco at La Cabana in Astoria. It's amazing—a slab of cheese cooked until it's soft, topped with onions and cilantro. The green sauce is key.

Street cart in Queens: The Arepa Lady because they are ridiculously delicious.

Dessert/ bakery in Queens: I'm a big fan of La Guli for their carrot cake, zeppoles, sfingi, cassata cake, and homemade gelato.

Specialty food spot: Parrot Market for the extensive Eastern European foodstuffs, including a sweet-yeasted Hungarian bread stuffed with nuts and chocolate.

Other: Rincon Criollo in Corona for the Ropa Vieja comes to mind. The doubles at Singh's Roti Shop are also amazing.

The Pepsi-Cola sign in Long Island City. *(photo by Andrea Lynn)*

Poussin au Pot at M. Wells Dinette.
(photo by Janis Turk)

LONG ISLAND
CITY

The schoolhouse-vibe interior of
M. Wells Dinette, located inside
MoMA's PS1. *(photo by Janis Turk)*

LONG ISLAND CITY

Long Island City is a hodgepodge of industrial space, television and film studios, new high-rise apartment buildings just steps from the water and, in recent years, a cluster of restaurants to feed this growing residential and working population. While the Pepsi-Cola sign on the East River harkens to the more industrial days of LIC, the area has evolved into the trendiest scene in the borough. Serving up locally grown comfort food in an old-fashioned store setting, **Sage General Store** gained NYC notoriety from its homemade spin on the Hostess cupcake, and has been featured on the Food Network's *Diners, Drive-ins and Dives* for its beyond-cheesy mac and cheese. **Tournesol** is a classic French bistro, offering traditional staples like steak frites. At **M. Wells Dinette**, a husband-and-wife team run what they refer to as "Quebeco-American" cuisine, serving up a menu of ever-changing creations like snails and a French-Canadian meat pie, *tourtiére*, that *The New York Times* can't get enough of: "Those who recall the thrill of eating at the Momofuku restaurants for the first time would do well to book passage on the No. 7 train, bound for Hunters Point," wrote Sam Sifton. But the eclectic arrangement of food and bars isn't the only plus to Long Island City: make sure to take in the breathtaking, unadulterated view of the Manhattan skyline, too.

FOOD SHOP: Slovak Czech Varieties

Sure, Slovak Czech Varieties gives a fascinating glimpse into imported food products of the region, but that's not their only shining glory. Linger over the selection of adorable European handmade wooden toys and stock up for future unique birthday or holiday gifts for the kids. These toys were the store's primary seller when they opened, but the decision to include imported Eastern European food soon added quite the boost to sales. On the food front, popular items at this decade-old shop include Czech and Hungarian-style salamis, Popradsky teas, and divine Horalky chocolate wafers. Other Eastern European finds are candies, pickles, and the unique Slovak sheep cheese Bryndza. Swing by on Saturdays and Sundays for the weekend-only Czech cooked dumpling loaf, usually potato-based and fashioned into a loaf shape, boiled, and sliced to serve.

SLOVAK CZECH VARIETIES
Info: 1059 Jackson Ave.; 718-752-2093; slovczechvar.com
See You There: Take the 7 train to the Vernon Blvd.-Jackson Ave. stop.

M. Wells Dinette

The first time one of Hugue Dufour's culinary concoctions danced on my palate was during the first GoogaMooga Celebration. His fois gras—stuffed grilled cheese and horse bologna sandwich was a revolution and the one bright spot in the unorganized confusion of this Brooklyn food and music festival. The sandwich is everything it sounds like: overindulgent, potentially sky-high cholesterol inducing, and one of the most wildly delicious, inventive sandwiches I've ever had. This description sums up the M. Wells Dinette experience, too. Set up in MoMA PS1, the hipster-feeling space pays homage to its former schoolhouse past with mini chalkboard menus and desks for seating.

M. Wells Dinette is the second restaurant from Quebec-raised Hugue and his wife, Sarah Obraitis, who remain devoted to changing the cuisine scene in Queens. Their previous creation, M. Wells, became the darling of the food world until a rumored too-high rent forced their closure. More than a year later, M. Wells Dinette came back housed in the art space to give a peek inside Dufour's creative mind. Open for brunch until 6 p.m. on weekends and noon until

6 p.m. Wednesdays through Friday, the lunch-only menu is luscious yet stick-to-your-ribs fare. Schedule a visit to the restaurant along with a stroll through the art collection and Long Island City scene. If you're craving a dinner option, venture to the couple's newest space: a reconstructed auto garage celebrating Hugue's creative twist on a steakhouse at M. Wells Steakhouse on 43-15 Crescent Street in Long Island City.

M. WELLS DINETTE
Info: 22-25 Jackson Ave., Long Island City; 718-786-1800; momaps1.org/about/mwells

See You There: Take the 7 train to the 45th Rd./ Court House Square stop or the E or M train to the 23rd St./Ely Ave. stop; Walk South on 23rd Street and make a right onto Jackson Avenue to MoMA PS 1. Just tell the front desk that you're restaurant-bound for a sticker to gain admission.

Insider Tip: With an ever-changing menu, it's difficult to pinpoint what to order. Ask the waiter to divulge the menu's current bestsellers for the best glimpse of what your meal should be.

Liver and Onions

Yield: 4 servings

This isn't the liver and onions of your childhood (or was it just my mom who plagued me with the dish?). Obraitis says this has been a hit on the menu, especially from skeptics (including myself). Almost charred on the outside yet silky inside, it's unlike any liver dish I've experienced before. The restaurant uses veal liver which is much harder to find, so I swapped it out with beef. If you can find veal liver, give it a try. Recipe adapted from M. Wells Dinette.

  1 pound slab bacon, cubed into 1-inch pieces
  5 large onions, thinly sliced
  2 garlic cloves, thinly sliced
  1 bottle red wine, such as Pinot Noir
  ½ cup sweet vermouth
  1½ tablespoons canola oil
  4 (6-ounce) beef livers, cleaned
  Kosher salt and freshly ground pepper

In a large nonstick skillet over medium-high heat, cook the onions and bacon until they sweat. Stir constantly and cook about

10 minutes. Reduce the heat if necessary to keep from getting any color on the onion. Add garlic slices, stirring and cooking about 1 minute. Add the bottle of wine, bring mixture to a boil over high heat, and let liquid reduce until almost dry, about 20 to 25 minutes. Add the vermouth and season with salt and pepper to taste. Cover to keep warm until serving.

Season liver with salt and pepper on both sides. Warm oil in a large sauté pan over medium-high heat, and sear the liver until it is medium rare, about 2 to 3 minutes per side, depending on the liver's thickness. (Touching the liver with your fingers is one of the best indicators to tell if it's medium-rare. You want the liver to feel like the bridge of skin between your thumb and index finger.) Place the liver on top of the onions and serve.

Poussin au Pot ■■■■■■■■■■■■■■■■■■■
Yield: 4 servings ■■■■■■■■■■■■■■■■■■

Move over roasted chicken, there's a new go-to chicken dish for entertaining. When buying the chicken, ask the butcher to debone it. M. Wells mixes this dish up with seasonal vegetables, like radishes and asparagus in the spring and mushrooms in the fall. If some of the stuffing oozes out of the chicken, all is not lost. Just scoop it up and serve it over the poussin. Also, don't throw out the broth; it's been infused with a ton of flavor and is an excellent excuse to make matzo balls (page 52). Recipe adapted from M. Wells Dinette.

1 slice white bread, cubed
¼ cup heavy cream
¼ pound ground pork
1 large egg
1 onion, finely minced
1 carrot, finely minced
1 celery stalk, finely minced
1 clove garlic, minced
1 tablespoon lemon zest (from about 2 large lemons)
Kosher salt and freshly ground pepper
16 cups chicken broth, or water
1 deboned (3-pound) chicken
1 cup chopped seasonal vegetables

In a medium bowl, add bread and cream; let the cubes soak for a few minutes. Add pork and egg into the bowl, mixing to combine. Set aside. In a large sauté pan over medium-high heat, add onion, carrot, and celery. Stirring constantly, cook until onions are softened and translucent, about 8 to 10 minutes. Add garlic, stirring and cooking until golden, about 30 seconds. Remove from heat, and season with lemon zest, salt, and pepper. Set aside to cool.

Meanwhile, in a large stockpot, bring the chicken broth to a boil. Once the onion mixture has cooled, add the ground pork to the vegetables and mix well. Use your hands to stuff the inside of the chicken with the pork mixture, making sure not to overstuff (or the chicken will not be able to close). Use butcher's twine to tie both sides of the chicken: start with the chicken legs first, so that the stuffing stays inside. Make sure the chicken is tied as tightly as possible, so the stuffing doesn't leak out. Using tongs, lower the stuffed chicken into the boiling broth, making certain the chicken is fully submerged in broth (adding more broth or water if necessary). Poach until chicken is cooked through, about 30 minutes, to an internal temperature of 165°F. Add the vegetables into the boiling chicken stock, and cook until al dente, just 1 or 2 minutes. Use a slotted spoon to remove vegetables and tongs to remove the chicken. Serve chicken on a platter surrounded by vegetables.

Sage General Store

As soon as you walk into Long Island City's Sage General Store, you'll notice the restaurant's guiding principles: employee T-shirts boast slogans like "Bacon. Better Than a Girlfriend" and "Locally Grown." And this isn't false advertising: Sage General uses locally sourced ingredients and products, and its menu is a twist on American comfort food, revolving around that pork favorite, bacon. (There's even a swoon-worthy bacon-enhanced brownie.) In fact, Sage General put "locavore" food on the horizon even before Manhattan became abuzz with eating locally. And don't miss their homemade spin on the Hostess cupcake.

It was eating her way through Europe that gave Leslie an early foray into the world of cuisine. This translated into private catering gigs and a move with her husband to Italy, famous for local open-air produce markets. Cooking and baking everything from scratch with market-fresh ingredients inspired Leslie to open her own company back in New York City. In 1998, a three-seat lunch spot was born in Long Island City, which relied on local ingredients. Now located for the past few years at a larger location, they are a good-size restaurant plus a thriving catering business. Besides getting produce from local area farmers' markets, she also reaps the organic goodness from Brooklyn Grange's nearby organic rooftop farm (which, despite its name, is located in Long Island City).

Sage General is a catering fixture in the community. Twenty years ago, Leslie's first catering client was **Sesame Street**; the show still requests food from her today. In fact, she provided the healthy vegetarian fare for First Lady Michelle Obama's visit to the set. Nilsson also supplies eats to Silvercup Studios, which fed the casts of **The Sopranos**, **Sex and the City**, **30 Rock**, and **Gossip Girl**. "When I first came out here, I loved the fact that all the movie productions were out here, and they became our best customers," Nilsson said. But now, one of her favorite aspects of the area is the ethnic diversity of the neighborhood. "There's a phenomenal amount of diversity among ethnic food, of which we are not one. There's always some little mom and pop shop to discover," she said.

Sage General Store's steak sandwich gets so much glory from customers that the restaurant can't take it off the menu. Served on flatbread, the grilled flank steak is served with caramelized onions, watercress, and spicy chipotle mayonnaise. Another fan fave is the Monterey Vegetable Sandwich with avocado, marinated cucumbers, arugula, and Jack cheese on 7-grain bread. Guy Fieri's **Diners, Drive-ins and Dives** profiled the spot, featuring their divine homey spin on mac and cheese. And Sage is a trendsetter, too: It was Leslie's pregnancy cravings for a Hostess cupcake that prompted the creation of a homemade version, which started a wave of cupcake imitation throughout Manhattan.

(photo by Janis Turk)

Sage General Store's most popular dessert: the homemade Hostess cupcake.

(photo by Janis Turk)

As far as where Leslie eats locally, for an Asian fix, she's a big fan of Shi right by the water. For Italian food, she loves the family run Manducatis, and its sister restaurant, Manducatis Rustica.

SAGE GENERAL STORE
Info: 24-20 Jackson Ave.; 718-361-0707; sagegeneralstore.com

See You There: Take the 7 train to the 45th Rd./Court House Square stop or the E or the M train to the 23rd St./ Ely Ave. stop. The restaurant is practically across from the Citibank building.

For an authentic experience: The restaurant has garnered acclaim for their roasted chicken, mac and cheese, pizzas from a wood-burning oven, and famous homemade spin on the Hostess cupcake, of course.

Kale Salad with Almonds, Anchovy Dressing, and Parmesan

Yield: 4 servings

The most time-consuming part of this recipe is cleaning and chopping the kale, which can be done way in advance of dinner. Also, make sure to use the salad spinner to dry the kale the best you can. The drier the kale is, the better the dressing can cling to it. Recipe adapted from Sage General Store.

    1 bunch kale (about 1 pound)
    ⅓ cup sliced almonds
    3 anchovy fillets
    2 ½ tablespoons fresh lemon juice
    ¼ cup extra-virgin olive oil
    ¼ pound good-quality Parmesan cheese

To prepare kale, remove the kale leaves from the stem, discarding stems. Layer a few kale leaves on top of each other, roll into a circular shape and thinly slice to julienne. Place chopped kale into a large bowl (you should have around 8 cups of chopped kale).

In a medium sauté pan over high heat, warm and add almonds. Stirring occasionally but always keeping a watchful eye on the almonds, cook until golden and toasted, about 3 to 5 minutes.

Chop the anchovy fillets into small pieces. Use the back of a knife to mash the pieces into a pastelike consistency. Add the anchovy paste into a small bowl along with lemon juice. Whisk together, pouring the oil into the dressing. (In addition, if the anchovy is still too chunky, use an immersion blender to smooth it out.) Toss the kale with the dressing in the large bowl, adding the almonds into the salad to combine. Then, using a Microplane, make a pillowy layer of grated Parmesan on top of the salad. (Use as much cheese as you'd like; I err on the side of too much!) Serve.

The much-requested Kale Salad at Sage General Store. *(photo by Janis Turk)*

Mac and Cheese ■■■■■■■■■■■■■■■
Yield: 6 to 8 servings ■■■■■■■■■■■■■■■

Sage General Store makes no qualms about one of the secrets to their spectacular mac and cheese: They use all artisanal cheeses. And then there's the five-cheese combination (cheddar, Monterey Jack, fontina, blue, and goat) that provide the creamy texture and distinctive taste that they wanted to achieve. They won't give out the exact proportions, so this was the mixture I came up with while trying to replicate it. Feel like experimenting? Use 8 ounces of aged cheddar mixed with almost 1 pound of artisanal cheeses of your own selection. Recipe adapted from Sage General Store.

    1 pound elbow macaroni
    ½ cup (1 stick) unsalted butter
    1 medium onion, diced (about 1/2 cup)
    ½ teaspoon kosher salt
    ¼ teaspoon freshly ground pepper
    2 ½ cups heavy cream
    8 ounces aged Vermont cheddar (such as Cabot), shredded
    4 ounces artisanal Monterey Jack cheese, roughly chopped
    4 ounces artisanal fontina cheese, roughly chopped
    4 ounces artisanal blue cheese, roughly chopped
    2 ounces artisanal goat cheese
    1 cup Panko bread crumbs
    ¼ teaspoon ground cayenne powder

Heat oven to 350°F. Prepare a 9 x 12-inch casserole dish by greasing it. Bring a large pot of water to a boil over high heat. When boiling, add macaroni, and cook until al dente as specified by the package (usually about 7 minutes). When cooked, drain in a colander, but don't rinse with water (you want those pasta starches to stay on the macaroni).

Meanwhile, in a large saucepan over medium-high heat, melt butter. Add onion, salt, and pepper, and cook, stirring with a heat-proof spatula, until onions are golden brown, about 6 to 8 minutes. Add heavy cream and bring to a simmer, stirring constantly. Reduce heat to medium, add all the cheeses, and stir constantly until a majority of the cheese has melted. Remove from heat, and add macaroni into the sauce, stirring well to combine. Transfer into the prepared casserole dish. In a small bowl, mix bread crumbs and cayenne. Sprinkle bread crumbs over the top of the mac and cheese.

Cover mac and cheese with foil and bake 30 minutes. Remove foil and continue baking for an additional 20 to 30 minutes or until golden brown on top. Remove from oven, let cool slightly, and serve.

Long Island City Walking Tour

Take the 7 train from Manhattan to Vernon Boulevard-Jackson Avenue. Walk to 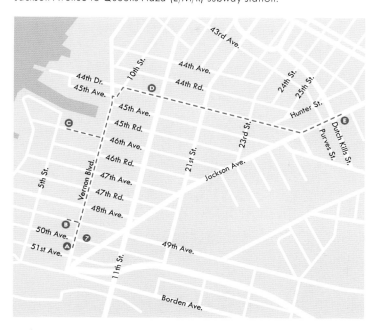 **Tournesol** (50-12 Vernon Blvd.; 718-472-4355) and treat yourself to a French feast, splitting your choice of mussels and frites, croque monsieur, or tarragon-bathed escargot. Continue north on Vernon Boulevard, make a left on 49th Avenue to **Casa Enrique** (5-48 49th Ave.) for their raved-about guacamole, plus Mexican-French fusion dishes. Head back to Vernon and make a left. If it's a summer weekend, make a left on 46th Avenue and check out the **LIC Flea & Food** (5-25 46th Ave.), where mostly Queens-based restaurants, shops, and food companies offer just a hint of what they provide (my personal favorite are the artisan marshmallows from MitchMallows in flavors like BLT or banana split). Otherwise, continue on Vernon and make a right on 44th Drive to **John Brown Smokehouse** (10-43 44th Dr.; 347-617-1120). Eater (rightly so) declared their Burnt Ends sandwich as one of the best in NYC. Continue on 44th Drive for three blocks and make a left on Jackson Avenue for **Dutch Kills** (27-24 Jackson Ave.). Open after 5 p.m., Dutch Kills beckons with a speakeasy-style and a not-too-expansive drink menu. But that's okay. Just tell the mixologist your favorite liquors and cocktails, and they'll handcraft a specialty drink tailored to your taste buds. Continue on Jackson Avenue to Queens Plaza (E/M/R) subway station.

The famous aerosol graffiti at 5Pointz, which was whitewashed in November 2013. *(photo by Janis Turk)*

Exterior of Eddie's Sweet Shop.
(photo by Janis Turk)

FOREST HILLS/
REGO PARK

Raspberry linzer tarts from Andre's Hungarian Bakery. *(photo by Janis Turk)*

FOREST HILLS/REGO PARK

I fell a little in love with the huge raspberry linzer tarts at **Andre's Hungarian Bakery**: raspberry jam sandwiched between flaky, buttery pastry rounds and dusted with powdered sugar that left a trail on my clothes no matter how gentle my bite was. I went so overboard with my linzer tart purchase that the lady helming the counter threw in a handful of rugelach. Later in the day, I tasted the nut-and-raisin-filled cookies, amazed at their deliciousness (and that I had almost missed out on them).

I still had that bag of pastries (and much more to lug) with me as I tried to get a cab on Metropolitan Avenue in Forest Hills, which is more difficult than one might think. So happy for a cab after at least twenty minutes of failed attempts, I asked the driver if he wanted any cookies, and handed over a few rugelach. "I know where these are from," he exclaimed in an "aha" moment. He told me how years ago, he took a Queens couple—the wife had survived the Holocaust and Auschwitz—to Brooklyn for a meal. He waited for them to eat and gave them a return ride to Queens. The couple was so grateful for this lovely gesture that they had him stop at Andre's, so they could buy him what they said was the finest rugelach anywhere. The cab driver had devoured the rugelach but later forgot the bakery's name. He never forgot the taste though, and to his delight, I'd just jolted his memory.

That's only one of many nostalgic charms of the Forest Hills/Rego Park area. The area's Jewish population relies on the three-generation-owned **Ben's Best Kosher Deli** for a fix of matzo ball soup and a pastrami sandwich. Ben's is just as good as its more famous Manhattan counterparts, but thankfully isn't overflowing with tourists. Take a step back in time at **Eddie's Sweet Shop**, a century-old soda fountain shop with classic egg creams, malts, and ice cream sundaes. Add a walk through Forest Hills Gardens to build up an appetite for your next food adventure.

Pastrami sandwich and celery soda at Ben's Best Kosher Deli. (photo by Janis Turk)

Ben's Best Kosher Deli

What was once a mainstay has turned into a rarity in New York—the classic Jewish deli. According to Ben's Best owner, Jay Parker, around seventy years ago there were about two thousand Jewish delis. That number has dwindled to sixteen in recent years. Skip the wraparound lines in Manhattan and go straight to Ben's Best, which many say has the best pastrami sandwich in the city due to its cured-by-hand process There's also pastrami- or corned beef–filled knishes and brisket slices piled high on garlic bread.

Parker's grandfather, the famous Benjamin, opened the deli in 1945 in the Bronx before moving to Jewish-concentrated Rego Park. Jay Parker became the third-generation owner in the early eighties, deciding to give the family business a whirl after his grandfather's death and a successful stint in the financial industry. Whatever you order, from the large, crisped potato latkes, to the silky chopped liver, it's like a Jewish grandmother is slaving away in the kitchen for your eating pleasure. So live it up—and order your choice of Dr. Brown's soda to pair with the meal; it's popular in delis because it was the only kosher soda before Coca-Cola received its certification. Make sure to alert Parker if it will be your first taste of Dr. Brown's Cel-Ray Soda; he enjoys snapping photos when someone sips the celery-flavored soft drink for the first time. Ben's Best also doesn't mind giving a crash course in the cuisine; such was the case last year when they hosted the 2013 Scripps National Spelling Bee Champion, Queens native Arvind Mahankali, who won on the word *knaidel*, Yiddish for matzo ball, yet had never tasted one before.

BEN'S BEST KOSHER DELI
Info: 96-40 Queens Blvd., Rego Park; 718-897-1700

See You There: Take the R train into Forest Hills to the 63rd Dr./Rego Park stop. Walk east on Queens Blvd. for about 1 block.

For an Authentic Experience: All the items are family recipes, so you can't go wrong with anything you order. Try the Chopped Chicken Liver, Fried Kreblach, Chicken Soup (with noodles, matzo balls, or kreblach), or Corned Beef or Pastrami Sandwich.

Stuffed Cabbage with Tomato-Raisin Sauce
Yield: about 12 cabbage rolls (4 servings)

The original recipe given to me by Ben's Best Deli called for two cabbages, but I realized the impossibility of boiling two cabbages at the same time unless you own two very large stockpots (one for each head of cabbage). I have almost every kitchen utensil and equipment under the sun, but even I only have one stockpot. Get a cabbage on the large side (4 to 5 pounds) because you'll need all those leaves. Also, this recipe isn't for the culinary faint of heart. It takes 1 hour to boil the cabbage and 2 hours to cook the rolls, and that's not including preparation time. But the results are worth it: a hearty, stick-to-your-ribs sweet yet tangy tomato sauce over tender cabbage filled with beef and rice. Recipe adapted from Jay Parker.

FOR THE CABBAGE ROLLS

1 (4- to 5-pound) green cabbage
1 tablespoon canola oil
1 medium yellow onion, chopped
2 pounds 80-percent lean/20-percent fat ground beef
½ teaspoon kosher salt
¼ teaspoon freshly ground pepper
1 teaspoon garlic powder
½ teaspoon ground cumin
½ cup uncooked rice
⅓ cup ketchup
2 large eggs

FOR THE SAUCE

1 cup tomato paste
1 cup tomato purée
1 cup canned jellied cranberry sauce
¼ cup lemon juice
¼ cup white vinegar
½ cup raisins
½ cup chopped dried apricots
½ cup granulated sugar
½ teaspoon kosher salt
2 cinnamon sticks

Use a knife to core the cabbage. Add cabbage to a large stockpot and fill almost to the top with water. Bring to a boil over high heat, and let cabbage cook for 1 hour. The cabbage will want to float, so set a large sauté pan on top of the stockpot to prevent cabbage from floating.

Meanwhile, prepare the sauce: In a medium heavy-duty pot, add all the sauce ingredients, and bring to a boil over high heat. Cover, reduce heat to low, and let sauce cook for 30 minutes. Use a whisk to stir the ingredients together, especially to break up the cranberry sauce. Cover again, and cook 30 more minutes. Remove from heat, taste, and adjust seasonings if needed.

Meanwhile, drain cooked cabbage in a colander, letting cold water run over it to cool the cabbage. In a large sauté pan, warm oil over medium-high heat. Add onion, and cook until softened, about 5 to 7 minutes, stirring occasionally. Add ground beef, continuing to stir to break up meat, and season with salt, pepper, garlic powder, and cumin. Sauté until meat is fully cooked, about 5 minutes. Stir in the rice, letting it cook in the beef fat for 1 to 2 minutes. Add in ketchup, stir to combine, and remove from heat. Transfer mixture to a large bowl, and let cool for a few minutes.

Stir eggs into the meat, mixing to combine.

Preheat oven to 350°F. Remove 2 cabbage leaves, trimming off any thick stem pieces. Put the 2 cabbage leaves on top of each other, adding about ¼ cup meat mixture into the center of the cabbage leaves. Roll the leaves, tucking in the excess leaves on both sides, like you would roll a burrito. Fit into the baking pan. Repeat, until the meat mixture is finished, making about 12 cabbage rolls. Pour the reserved sauce over the cabbage rolls, cover with foil, and place in preheated oven. Cook until rice is cooked and cabbage leaves are tender, about 2 hours. Remove from oven, and serve.

Latkes (Potato Pancakes)
Yield: about 10 pancakes

I always thought the key to the perfect potato pancake was hand-grating the potatoes and onion versus using a food processor. But Ben's Best Deli says the real trick is using paper towels to soak up the excess liquid of the grated potato and onion. Put a double layer of paper towels together, and press down on the grated mixture, repeating a few times until a majority of the liquid has been removed. The trick is not to go overboard (like my husband did as he tried to dry the grated potatoes like his life depended on it) or it will be too dry. The latkes are much larger at Ben's Best, but I cut down on the size to make them more sauté pan-friendly and to avoid having to use a deep fryer. Recipe adapted from Jay Parker.

    1 pound russet potatoes (about 2 medium potatoes)
    1 medium yellow onion
    Canola oil, as needed
    1 large egg
    1 teaspoon kosher salt
    ¼ teaspoon freshly ground pepper
    1 teaspoon baking powder
    ½ cup all-purpose flour
    ½ cup matzo meal
    Sour cream or applesauce (or both!), to serve

Grate the potatoes and onion in the food processor, or by using a box grater fitted inside a large bowl. Using paper towels, press down on the grated mixture to remove the excess liquid. According to Ben's Best Deli, the more liquid you can remove, the more awesome the latkes will taste (and I agree).

Meanwhile, in a large skillet, warm ½-inch of oil over medium-high heat. Add egg, salt, pepper, and baking powder to potato-onion mixture, stirring with a fork or spatula to combine. Then, mix flour and matzo meal into the mixture until well combined.

The oil is hot enough to be used when a small amount of potato pancake mixture is dropped into the oil and it bubbles immediately. To cook the potato pancakes, drop 1/4 cup of mixture into the hot oil. Using a spatula, press down on pancakes to flatten as much as possible. Cook until golden brown (about 3 to 5 minutes), flip with spatula, and cook until pancakes are golden-brown on remaining side. Using a spatula, transfer cooked potato pancakes to a paper towel–lined plate, and repeat until you've used all of the mixture. Reduce heat to medium if the second batch of potato pancakes is browning too quickly. Sprinkle additional salt on top of pancakes, if desired, and serve with sour cream and/or applesauce.

Matzo Ball Soup ■ ■ ■ ■
Yield: 4 servings ■ ■ ■ ■ ■ ■

Jay Parker says he uses seltzer in this recipe because the carbonation aids in the rising of the matzo ball dough. The matzo balls are best when floating in home-made chicken soup with diced carrots and feathery dill sprigs. Recipe adapted from Jay Parker.

4 large eggs, slightly beaten
¼ cup canola oil
¼ cup seltzer
1 cup matzo meal
1 teaspoon kosher salt, divided
½ teaspoon freshly ground pepper
6 to 8 cups chicken stock (homemade, if possible)
Chopped dill, to serve (optional)

Place eggs, oil, seltzer, matzo meal, ½ teaspoon salt, and pepper in large bowl. Using a fork, mix well, cover, and then refrigerate for 1 hour.

Fill a large pot with water and remaining ½ teaspoon salt and bring to a boil over high heat. After water has come to a boil, reduce the flame to low so water is simmering. Remove matzo ball dough from the refrigerator and make golf ball–sized balls. (Wet your hands with water to prevent sticking.) Add the matzo balls to the simmering water. Cover with a lid and cook for 30 minutes. Take pot off the heat, but keep it covered and let it cool for 10 minutes. The matzo balls should be tender when poked with a fork. Heat the chicken stock in a medium pot. To serve, add chicken stock into a bowl, along with matzo balls. Garnish with chopped dill and serve.

Eddie's Sweet Shop

Walking into Eddie's Sweet Shop is almost akin to finding a miniature Willy Wonka world in Queens. People happily perched on swivel stools, hot fudge sauce melting over ice cream scoops, homemade fizzy drinks, and candy galore. More than ninety years old, Eddie's Sweet Shop is a step into soda history.

The old-school interior of Eddie's Sweet Shop. (photo by Janis Turk)

Vito Citrano's family is the fourth line of owners, having run the restaurant since 1968. "We make our own toppings, ice cream, whipped cream, everything—it's all homemade on the premises," he says. "Families that have been coming for years; their grandparents brought them and now they're bringing their kids."

To order at Eddie's Sweet Shop, you have to know the old-time ordering lingo. "It's confusing to new customers. That's how we know if you're new or not," says Vito. An ice cream soda has ice cream, homemade syrup (like fruit, root beer, or Coke) and seltzer, while a float is a milkshake plopped with a scoop or two of ice cream. A root beer soda or root beer float used to go by the moniker of Brown Cow, and a Broadway was coffee ice cream plunked into chocolate soda.

Then there's the mystery of the egg cream, which contains neither egg nor cream. Vito says there are so many stories about the origins of the name, like the one saying egg (probably just the whites) was incorporated into the drink to make it frothy. His favorite tale is that the inventor of the egg cream named the drink after himself, which was a very hard-to-pronounce German name. The name was similar-sounding to "egg cream" and just turned into that over time.

Vito can't narrow down a top choice on the Eddie's Sweet Shop menu: "If there's something that's not my favorite, it won't be on the menu," he quips. His ice creams differ from his competitors'—a coffee ice cream that offers subtleness versus a caffeinated jolt, and his tropical play of pistachio pineapple. You'll just have to graze your way through the selection and decide on your own favorite.

EDDIE'S SWEET SHOP
Info: 105-29 Metropolitan Ave., Forest Hills; 718-520-8514

See You There: Take the E, M, or R train into Forest Hills to the 71st Ave. stop. Walk southwest on 71st Ave. (which will change into Continental Ave.) for about 10 to 15 minutes. Make a left on Manse St. and then a right on 72nd Rd. It's a bit of a walk, but it's a lovely one in pleasant weather—you go through the greenery of Forest Hills Gardens, not believing you're still in NYC. Restaurants can call a cab to get you back to the subway, if desired.

For an Authentic Experience: Vito says to order—what else?—a hot fudge sundae: great ice cream, homemade hot fudge, and delectable whipped cream. Vito says the best syrups are chocolate and root beer.

Strawberry Ice Cream Soda at Eddie's Sweet Shop. *(photo by Janis Turk)*

An Egg Cream at Eddie's Sweet Shop. *(photo by Janis Turk)*

Egg Cream

Yield: 1 drink

The only clue I could get from Vito was that the chocolate syrup used in the egg cream contains chocolate. No family soda secrets are dished out at Eddie's Sweet Shop. "We feel like we're like Coca-Cola in that sense," laughs Vito. But this classic New York concoction is a blend of milk, seltzer, and chocolate syrup. To bring this up a notch and make it a chocolate ice cream soda, mix together the chocolate syrup and a scoop of chocolate ice cream and top with seltzer.

FOR THE HOMEMADE CHOCOLATE SYRUP

1 1/2 cups water

1 cup good-quality natural-process
    unsweetened cocoa powder

3/4 cup granulated sugar

2 tablespoons corn syrup

1 1/2 teaspoons vanilla extract

1/2 cup chocolate chip morsels
    (dark chocolate or semi-sweet)

FOR THE EGG CREAM

1/2 cup whole milk

1/4 cup homemade chocolate syrup or
    store-bought chocolate syrup

Seltzer, as needed

Make the chocolate syrup: In a medium, heavy-duty pot, combine the water, cocoa powder, sugar, corn syrup, and vanilla extract. Bring to a boil over high heat, and let boil until thickened, about 2 to 4 minutes, whisking vigorously to combine. Remove from the heat, and stir in chocolate chips until completely melted. Let cool. Refrigerate in a covered container for up to 7 days. (There will be about 1 cup of chocolate syrup left over for additional egg creams.)

Make the egg cream: In a 10- to 12-ounce glass, stir together the milk and chocolate syrup to thoroughly combine. Slowly pour in the seltzer. Gently stir again if needed.

Strawberry Ice Cream Soda ■ ■ ■ ■ ■ ■ ■ ■ ■ ■
Yield: 1 drink ■ ■ ■ ■ ■ ■ ■ ■ ■ ■ ■ ■ ■ ■ ■ ■ ■

I chose to use frozen strawberries versus fresh because they're available year-round and are more dependable for sweetness.

FOR THE STRAWBERRY SYRUP
1 (16-ounce) bag frozen strawberries
 (sliced or whole), thawed
½ tablespoon freshly squeezed lemon juice
½ cup water
⅓ cup granulated sugar

FOR THE STRAWBERRY ICE CREAM SODA
¼ cup strawberry syrup
½ cup vanilla ice cream
 (or any other complementary flavor)
Seltzer, as needed

Make the strawberry soda: In a medium pot, combine the strawberries (including any juice from the thawed strawberries), lemon juice, water, and sugar. Bring to a boil over high heat, and stir to dissolve the sugar. Reduce heat to medium or medium-low and simmer for about 10 minutes. Remove from heat, and let cool. Transfer to a food processor, and purée the strawberry mixture. Refrigerate the syrup in a covered container for up to 5 days.

Make the strawberry ice cream soda: In a 10- to 12-ounce glass, stir together the syrup and ice cream to combine. Slowly pour in the seltzer. Stir again and serve.

Wafa's

Wafa Chami's adventure into the Middle Eastern restaurant business is equal parts talent, persistence, and luck. "I used to just invite a lot of friends to my house," she explained. "They loved the food. They always said that I'm an excellent cook and should open a restaurant. I've been working on it for more than twenty years."

Around five years ago, she rode on this encouragement to open a Lebanese counter in Forest Hills, soon striking up a partnership with her three sons, Youssef, Hussein, and Sharif. The popularity of the restaurant was exhilarating and eye-opening, and soon they needed a larger space to keep up with demand. So they sold the restaurant, lease, and equipment with their eye on another spot in Forest Hills.

But the owner of the perfect (and empty) restaurant spot wouldn't budge on the price, making it semi-elusive. Months went by, and the family began to think their restaurant dreams were over—until the owner finally caved. "It's very hard to find a place [in] a good area that's reasonably priced. This happened to be it. I guess the stars aligned," her sons agreed. Her sons say they can't pinpoint any popular menu items, mostly because everything gets ordered; there's nothing on the menu, in fact, that doesn't. A key to the restaurant's success, says Wafa—who prepares all the food herself—is that she cooks from the heart. "I like taking my time with everything," she says,. "After five years, I won't let anybody touch the food, only me. I have a helper but not to put the food together."

Her mantra is that everything is fresh and homemade: from the spectacular hot sauce that you can purchase to-go for perking up meals at home, to the cheese pie that's made from homemade yogurt, which Wafa works into homemade cheese. The lean beef used with lamb for the Lebanese specialty of kibbeh is hand-ground by Wafa into almost a cream cheese—like creaminess. And, of course, there's the extra dose of love that Wafa cooks into each item.

WAFA'S

Info: 100-05 Metropolitan Ave. (between 70th and 71st Aves.), Forest Hills; 718-880-2055; wafasfood.com

See You There: Take the E, M, or R train into Forest Hills to the 71st Ave. stop. Walk southwest on 71st Ave. (which will change into Continental Ave.) for about 10 to 15 minutes. Make a right onto Metropolitan Ave. and walk a couple blocks to the restaurant. Just like Eddie's Sweet Shop, it's a bit of a walk, but it's a lovely one in nice weather. Since you're so close, make a left from the restaurant and walk a few blocks on Metropolitan to 105-29 Metropolitan Ave. and have dessert at Eddie's. The restaurant can call a cab to take you back to the subway, if you're too stuffed to walk.

For an Authentic Experience: Let Wafa cook you an ultimate Middle Eastern spread: begin with hummus and the okra mezze, spinach pie, and cheese pie next, followed by mujadarah and kibbeh.

Okra and Tomato Mezze (front) and Mujadarah at Wafa's. *(photo by Janis Turk)*

Okra and Tomato Mezze

Yield: 4 servings

Wafa says okra skeptics don't want to try this mezze at first out of fear that the okra is slimy. But it's far from it. Wafa says the key is buying baby okra, which is almost impossible to buy fresh and even a little difficult in its frozen state. (The bigger the okra, the more prone it is to sliminess.) Luckily, I found cans of "young okra in tomato sauce" around Astoria that were just meant for this recipe. (They are also available for order at titanfoods.net.) Pomegranate juice adds an unexpected tang to the dish, which works well as a side dish to a meat entrée or an appetizer with pita wedges or pita chips. Recipe adapted from Wafa Chami.

1 tablespoon extra-virgin olive oil
1 medium onion, diced
3 cloves garlic, minced
1 cup cilantro leaves
2 (10-ounce) jars Palirria Young Okras in Tomato Sauce
2 medium tomatoes, chopped
¼ cup pomegranate juice
¼ cup water
½ teaspoon ground coriander
½ teaspoon red hot chili flakes
½ teaspoon kosher salt
Pita wedges, serving

Warm olive oil in a large sauté pan over medium-high heat. Add onion to the pan, and cook over medium-high heat, stirring occasionally until soft, about 5 minutes. Add garlic and cilantro, cooking about 1 minute until garlic is golden (but don't let it burn). Add okra with tomato sauce, tomatoes, pomegranate juice, water, and seasonings. Bring to a boil over high heat; reduce to medium and let mixture simmer for 10 minutes. Taste, adjusting seasonings if needed. Serve dip warm, cold, or at room temperature with pita wedges.

Substitution: It doesn't come out quite as well, but you can use 1 (16-ounce) bag frozen baby okra, thawed, if you can't find the jarred variety.

Mujadarah
Yield: 4 servings

When Wafa talks about adding a dose of love into her dishes, it's never more apparent than in her flavorful Mujadarah, a mix of caramelized onions, bulgur wheat, and lentils. Even though it's just a handful of ingredients, I couldn't get it "Wafa-perfect" even after many attempts. Wafa's lentils, olive oil, and bulgur wheat are all imported from Lebanon because she finds they're better quality, but she says Goya brand is an acceptable substitute. Recipe adapted from Wafa Chami.

2 tablespoons extra-virgin olive oil
4 large yellow onions, thinly sliced
1 cup green lentils
1 cup bulgur wheat
2 cups water

¼ teaspoon freshly ground pepper
½ teaspoon kosher salt
½ teaspoon ground cinnamon
½ teaspoon ground cumin
1 cup Greek yogurt with 1 tablespoon lemon zest, to serve

To make the caramelized onions: In a large sauté pan, warm olive oil over medium-high heat. Add onions, and reduce heat to medium-low. Cook onions until brown and caramelized, stirring occasionally, about 45 minutes. This isn't a quick process—more like a labor of love.

Meanwhile, add lentils to a medium pot and fill with water. Bring to a boil over high heat, and cook lentils until tender, about 15 to 20 minutes. Drain lentils in colander and rinse.

Back in the medium pot, stir in lentils, 1 cup bulgur wheat, half the caramelized onions, water, and seasonings. Bring to a boil over high heat, cover with a lid, and take off heat. Let sit for 10 to 15 minutes as bulgur wheat absorbs the water. Top with remaining caramelized onions and serve with a dollop of yogurt, if desired.

Cheburechnaya

A smattering of Bukharan Jews emigrating from Uzbekistan are in Rego Park, and represented in the kosher restaurant Cheburechnaya. Having no idea what to expect from a Russian restaurant with Asian influences, I soon swooned over the chebureki with meat (a combo of lamb and beef). A cross between a soup dumpling and an empanada, meat and juice spurts from the center of the large, flaky dough. "It's really hard to make at home," admits Miriam, who works at the restaurant owned by her uncle. "People tell me about trying to make it at home and it doesn't come out looking like ours because we have a deep fryer, a huge thing with a lot of oil in there. We throw it in and it comes out fluffy." For a walk on the more exotic side, Miriam says customers are crazy about the fried beef brains. "We had someone who took a video of my uncle cooking the brains, and he ate it and loved it so much that he took two orders to go. That's how much he loved the brains," she says.

The cuisine is also known for its Chinese-derived laghman noodles, which are twirled into soups or fried and smothered in honey for dessert. "It's supposed to be one long noodle piece, but we don't do that," admits Miriam. "We make the dough but have a machine to cut it because it's just a lot of work to cut."

CHEBURECHNAYA
Info: 92-09 63rd Dr.; 718-897-9080

How to Get There: Take the R or M train to the 63rd Dr. stop in Rego Park. Walk west on Queens Blvd. from the subway and make a left onto 63rd Dr.

Chak Chak, the dessert at Cheburechnaya, made from their homemade noodles smothered in honey and nuts. *(photo by Janis Turk)*

Forest Hills/Rego Park Walking Tour

Take the E or F train into Forest Hills, get off at the 75th Avenue stop and walk from Queens Boulevard to Ascan Avenue, where pizza aficionados flock to the wonder that is **Ⓐ Nick's Pizza** (108-26 Ascan Ave.; 718-263-1126). *New York* magazine remarked, "Owner Nick Angelis's light, fragrant, superbly charred crusts contrast beautifully with creamy fresh mozzarella—melted but not boiled over—and bright tomato sauce and basil." Loop back to Austin Street to **Ⓑ Cheese of the World** (71-48 Austin St.; 718-263-1933) and wander through their worldy fromage selection. Continue trekking down Austin Street. Make a right onto Continental Avenue and then walk one block to Queens Boulevard, making a left onto it. Welcome to the dessert extravaganza that is **Ⓒ Andre's Hungarian Bakery** (100-28 Queens Blvd.; 718-830-0266). Raves abound for the cherry strudel, but don't discount the rugelach and extra-large raspberry linzer tarts. Andre's Bakery is also given a shout-out in Nora Ephron's essay "The Lost Strudel or Le Strudel Perdu," where she's on an eternal quest for cabbage strudel, which apparently is only made by special request. Go next door to **Ⓓ Knish Nosh** (100-30 Queens Blvd.; 718-897-4456) and devour the knish of your choice—potato, sweet potato, spinach, meat, and more. They're rather large, so don't go overboard like I'm known to do. Continue to walk on Queens Boulevard in the same direction until you hit 66th Avenue; make a left onto it and turn onto Austin Street for **Ⓔ Rokhat Bakery** (65-43 Austin St.; 718-897-4493).

(photo by Janis Turk)

QUEENS FOOD PRO:
Famous Fat Dave, NYC Food Tour Guide

Why do you love Queens? The Ramones, who are from Forest Hills in Queens, sang, "New York City really has it all...OH OH OH OH YEAAAAAH." Well, they could just as easily have sang, "Queens really has it all." Queens has the biggest land mass of any of the five boroughs and if you think about it, it's the landmass that accounts for the amount of food. Those tall buildings in Manhattan don't have restaurants stacked up to the top floor. With all that space in Queens, there's plenty of room to serve all that diverse food. There are whole communities of people from places on Earth most Americans have never heard of. And the food is interesting at the least and life affirming at the best.

What's your Queens claim to food fame? I made myself famous, as in "Famous Fat Dave." That was sort of a joke. It was a reference to places like Nathan's Famous Hot Dogs or Queens' own Xi'an Famous Foods. Everyone in the food world is "famous" in New York, so it was sort of tongue-in-cheek. But I always demand people use my whole moniker of "Famous Fat Dave" if they aren't going to call me just Dave.

What do you think is the biggest misconception about Queens (food-related or not)? A lot of people assume that precisely *because* of all that diversity that can be found in Queens, it's not the place to go for more traditional New York City fare. People assume you'd better be eating Bhutanese goat cumin soup dumplings with a side of live drunken snails over sumac-infused baby bok choy or you're not getting the true Queens experience. But one of the entire city's juiciest burgers can be found at Donovan's Pub on Roosevelt Avenue. Easily one of my favorite slices of pizza comes out of the fiery hot, sixty-year-old brick oven at New Park in Howard Beach. Ben's Best Kosher Deli in Rego Park ranks up with the city's most delicious. Don't get me wrong, I love the post-1965 immigrant groups that brought the wild and crazy dishes we never dreamt of before. But Queens has some phenomenal old-school institutions that shouldn't be missed.

What's the most surprising experience (foodwise) you've had in Queens? I'm a Tony Bourdain fan. In his outer boroughs episode, he and David Chang of Momofuku fame visited a Korean barbecue restaurant in Flushing called Sik Gaek Chun Ha. They seemed to thoroughly enjoy plowing through piles of Korean-style shell fish and gleefully dumping the shells into a bin at their feet. It looked like my kind of spot! But the coup de grace, so to speak, was the cooking of a live octopus at their table. They knew that'd make controversial television, but if anything, the exotic cooking method enticed me even more. However, to my surprise, when I arrived at Sik Gaek Chun Ha and saw that live octopus on my table, I had a conscience about it. I know, I know. If you will eat an animal, you should be able to kill it. But, honestly, I don't think I could kill a cow unless he were trying to kill me first, and I eat plenty of beef. When the waitress put that octopus on the heat, I swear he reached out to me with his tentacles. That octopus knew what was happening. They are smart. I still ate it, but I would never do that again. I suppose I'm more of a softy than I thought I was.

What type of non-food activities do you recommend to others? I'd recommend going to the Jamaica Bay Wildlife Refuge in Broad Channel. I mean, bring a bagel sandwich from Bay Gull on Cross Bay Boulevard, so you don't starve to death while you're walking around. But that still counts as a non-food- related activity. You'd have no idea you were in the middle of New York City. If you go in spring, you'll see mama ducks walking alongside you with their ducklings in tow. If you go in fall, you'll see the leaves changing colors. The only giveaway that you are indeed in New York are the jumbo jets flying into and out of JFK nearby, and then the beautiful skyline of Manhattan in the distance once you've made it to the end of the path.

Let's say you had to move out of the country: What would be your last meal in Queens? What food establishment would you miss the most? Unless I had to move out of the country to take a job in Alexandria, Egypt, my last meal in Queens would be at Ali's Kabab Café on Steinway [in Astoria]. First of all, Ali is such a character, more than just a brilliant chef. I consider him a food historian, an Egyptian-American folk hero, and a friend. Just Ali's hummus and baba ghanoush appetizer plate sprinkled with sumac can make me swoon like a teenage girl catching a glimpse of Justin Bieber. The hibiscus tea he serves is the type that makes my eyelids droop shut and the muscles in my neck relax to the point where I can't seem to hold my head up straight. And I'm not even a tea drinker normally! So I always just ask Ali to cook me whatever he thinks is best for an entrée, and I'm never disappointed. Lamb cheeks, whole fish, even veal brains are all big winners in Ali's capable hands. He's not afraid to use a heavy hand when using those exotic Egyptian spices, so the flavor is distinct and it lights up my whole mouth. When I am gone from New York City for a while, I find myself dreaming of Ali's cooking. So I'd imagine that if, for some horrible reason, I had to move out of the country, I'd want Ali to cook my last meal in Queens.

A potato knish at Knish Nosh. *(photo by Janis Turk)*

Galdino Molinero helming the grill at Tortas Neza.
(photo by Andrea Lynn)

TORTAS TO

TORTAS M

TORTAS

TORTAS

TORTAS

- TUZO $ 8.
  PECHUGA
- POTROS 6
  ATLANTE
- POTOSINAS 8

CORONA

Manhattan's Little Italy has virtually disappeared, but Corona is still going strong with a slew of Italian gems. Family-owned and operated for eighty years, **Leo's Latticini**, along with Italian mainstays like **Park Side Restaurant**, offers a peek inside old-world Italian establishments. Inside, you'll find women fussing to make sure you feel at home in their restaurant and the familiar buzz of Italian being spoken. In recent years, a Mexican population has moved into the area, dishing out foil-wrapped, piping-hot tamales, dribble-worthy tortas on the street, like those from **Tortas Neza**, or homemade corn tortillas churned out during the nighttime hours at **Tortilleria Nixtamal**. All of this has merged Corona into an Italy-meets-Mexico food exploration with cannolis fit for an Italian grandmother alongside a secret-recipe specialty-made Mexican torta bread.

Leo's Latticini (also known as Mama's), is known for their Italian specialty sandwiches, like the roast-beef sandwich stuffed with cheese, peppers, and "gravy," which is actually a garlic-spiked oil and vinegar mixture. Observed by *The New York Times*, "What makes the heroes so special at Leo's is not simply the incredibly fresh mozzarella that comes out of the kitchen every morning or the crusty fresh bread or the meltingly tender roast pork Marie DeBenedittis makes as a special on Thursdays. It's also the warm welcome afforded everyone who comes into the store." **Tony's Pizzeria & Restaurant** is a casual joint with the most heavenly square of lasagna. And every meal should end with a great dessert, so venture over to the **Lemon Ice King of Corona**, featured on the opening of *The King of Queens* television show, with a selection of 60 flavors of Italian ices.

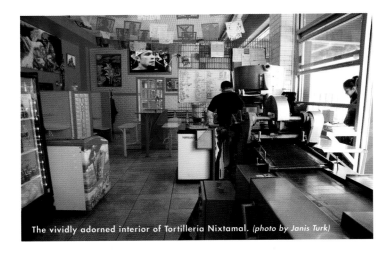

The vividly adorned interior of Tortilleria Nixtamal. *(photo by Janis Turk)*

Tortilleria Nixtamal

About four years ago, New York City began buzzing about a Queens-based tortilla factory that was supplying top-notch tortillas to area restaurants. The tortilla producer, Tortilleria Nixtamel, is the brainchild of owners Fernando Ruiz and Shauna Page. When the couple pondered why New York City didn't boast any good, authentic Mexican restaurants, Fernando realized the answer lay in the heavily processed manufactured tortillas used by most Mexican restaurants, unlike the sublime tortillas Ruiz enjoyed as a kid during visits to Mexico. Their goal was to produce from-scratch homemade tortillas, a practically nonexistent feat in a preservative-packed world. Rick Bayless, winner of *Bravo's Top Chef Masters*, raves about the quality of Tortilleria Nixtamal's tortillas.

The tortilla company began first, and soon they added a restaurant featuring those handcrafted tortillas. The process starts with corn from Illinois' Rovey Seed Farm Company, which is put through an Aztec method called nixtamal (hence the name) where the corn is partially cooked and soaked with calcium hydroxide (the dust from scraping limestone rock). The nixtamal is ground into masa, coarsely ground for tamales or kept whole for hominy in pozole. The freshness and attention to detail continues with the produce, which comes from Mexico to ensure authenticity. Meat, seafood, and cheeses are purchased from local purveyors in Queens, and the circle is complete as the tortillas are then sent all around New York City to restaurants like Pachanga Patterson in Astoria.

During dead-of-night restaurant off-hours, the tortilla press is in full use churning out thousands of tortillas with only half the workload. In addition to being a successful restaurant, Chef Santiago Barragan relies on his Puebla upbringing to make taco creations like grilled pork with pineapple (pastor), carrot-marinated chicken (pollo), chorizo, and more, along with enchiladas de mole and a layered meat, bean, and tortilla extravaganza called Sincronizada, among others. On one visit6, a man was enthusiastically eating the tres leches cake, claiming it was as good as his *madre*'s in Mexico. The staff, including Chef Santiago, say they're on a mission to prove Mexican food isn't all hard tacos stuffed with beef, tomatoes, and lettuce. Mission accomplished.

TORTILLERIA NÍXTAMAL
Info: 104-05 47th Ave., Corona; 718-699-2434; tortillerianixtamal.com

See You There: Take the 7 train into Queens to the 103rd St. stop. The restaurant is a short walk, just a handful of blocks away on 47th Ave.

Added Bonus: Corn products are available for retail; have a meal and buy tortillas or masa to go.

Salsa Roja
Yield: 2½ cups

Dried chiles, why have I not included you in my salsas all my life? I always reach for fresh chiles like jalapeño or poblano to infuse heat in my salsas, but the earthiness of the chipotle chiles and building heat of the puya chiles have converted me. If you can't find dried puya chiles, substitute the same amount of guajillo, which are very similar but not quite as high on the Scoville scale. A hearty swirl of this salsa into mashed avocados makes a heavenly guacamole. Recipe adapted from Chef Santiago Barragan.

6 plum tomatoes
4 to 6 dried chipotle chiles
4 dried puya chiles
2 medium cloves garlic
1 tablespoon chopped onion
¼ teaspoon kosher salt
⅛ teaspoon ground cumin powder
⅛ teaspoon ground allspice

Bring a medium pot of water to a boil over high heat. Score an "x" on the bottom of each tomato (which will help in the removal of the tomato skins), and remove the core. Add the tomatoes and dried chiles to the pot, and boil until chiles are tender, about 5 minutes. Using a slotted spoon, transfer the tomatoes and chiles to a bowl, and let cool for a few minutes before handling.

Chips and house salsas at Tortilleria Nixtamal. *(photo by Janis Turk)*

Meanwhile, in the bowl of a food processor, add garlic, onion, salt, cumin, and allspice. When cool enough to handle, remove peels from each tomato. Discard the peels, and add tomatoes into the food processor. Using a knife or kitchen shears, snip the stem off each chile, and cut along it sidewise to open it and remove the seeds. Place the seedless chiles into the food processor, and purée until blended and smooth, about 1 minute.

Barbacoa Lamb Tacos ■■■■■■■■■■■■■

Yield: about 8 tacos ■■■■■■■■■■■■■■

Barbacoa implies the technique of cooking meats over an open fire. And, yep, you guessed it, the better-known American word *barbecue* is derived from this. At Tortilleria Nixtamal, the lamb is wrapped in maguey leaves and steamed, which is a common modern-day equivalent of barbacoa in Mexico. According to Lesley Tellez, owner of Eat Mexico Culinary Tours, the maguey leaves perfume the meat with sweetness. Maguey leaves are hard to track down, so in this adaptation of the recipe, I braise the meat. The braising liquid contains the same spices the meat marinates in within the maguey leaves. While this recipe can still work without the maguey leaves, the epazote is a must. Tellez says, "It's único," adding that it can be found year-round in Latino markets. I discovered that my grocery store is stocked with epazote (although its pointy leaves are frequently mislabeled). If unable to find it fresh, order dried epazote online and substitute 2 tablespoons for the amount of fresh. Recipe adapted from Chef Santiago Barragan.

    1 tablespoon canola oil
    Kosher salt and freshly ground pepper, to taste
    2 to 2½ pounds lamb shoulder chops
    10 to 12 fresh thyme sprigs
    1 bunch fresh epazote
    2½ cups chicken broth
    8 cloves garlic, peeled
    1 teaspoon ground cumin
    8 small corn tortillas, to serve
    Chopped cilantro, to serve
    Chopped onions or scallions, to serve
    Sliced radishes, to serve
    Chopped jalapeños, to serve
    Salsa, to serve

In a large Dutch oven, warm oil over medium-high heat. Season the lamb generously with salt and pepper, add to the hot oil, and brown until golden on each side, about 4 minutes per side. (Do this in two batches if you can't get all the lamb in one layer.) Stir in thyme, epazote, chicken broth, garlic, cumin, and ½ teaspoon salt. Increase heat to high to bring mixture to a boil. Cover, and reduce heat to low, so the liquid is at a slow simmer. Cook until lamb is tender and able to shred into pieces with a fork, about 1½ hours.

When the lamb is tender, transfer meat to a bowl, and let cool. (Make sure to reserve the remaining cooking liquid.) Meanwhile, transfer thyme, epazote, and garlic to a cutting board. When both are slightly cooled, use a fork (or your hands) to remove the lamb meat from bones, and shred into pieces. Remove thyme leaves and epazote from their stalks, and mix in with the meat. Smash garlic, and add to meat, mixing to combine. Add a few tablespoons of the reserved cooking liquid, enough to moisten the meat.

To serve, briefly heat each tortilla on a pan over medium-high heat. Serve meat and tortillas with a plate of the condiments: cilantro, onions/scallions, radishes, and jalapeños. Let each person assemble their own taco to taste.

Shrimp Enchiladas (Enchiladas Camerones) ■■ ■■
Yield: 4 servings ■■■■■■■■■■■■■■■■■■

A drastically different version of enchiladas if you're used to Tex-Mex renditions, this Tortilleria Níxtamal recipe is drenched in a chile-based red sauce with a light shrimp filling. Just note that the tortillas must be warmed before rolling them, otherwise they will immediately crack and break. Also, these enchiladas are just begging to be served alongside refried beans. Recipe adapted from Chef Santiago Barragan.

FOR THE RED SAUCE
8 guajillo chiles
6 Chile de árbol chiles
½ teaspoon ground cinnamon
1 teaspoon ground cumin powder
2 cloves garlic
1 teaspoon dried thyme
½ teaspoon kosher salt
1 cup roughly chopped white onion
1 stick (½ cup) unsalted butter
1 cup white wine

FOR THE ENCHILADAS
2 teaspoons canola oil
1½ pounds medium shrimp
Corn tortillas, as needed
Chopped cilantro, to serve
Chopped onions, to serve
Sour cream, to serve
Queso fresco, to serve

Add the chiles into a medium pot filled with water. Bring to a boil over high heat, and cook until chiles are soft, about 8 to 10 minutes. Reserve 1 cup chile water. Remove stems from chiles (and the seeds also, for a milder sauce), and transfer chiles to a blender or food processor, along with the reserved chile water. Add the spices, garlic, and onion. Purée mixture until smooth.

Meanwhile, add butter to a medium pot. Warm over medium-high heat to melt the butter. Add chile mixture. Let sauce simmer over medium heat for 15 minutes. Taste, adjusting seasonings if needed.

Warm oil in a large skillet over high heat. Add shrimp, sautéing until pink and fully cooked, just a few minutes. Remove from heat, let cool slightly and chop shrimp into bite-size pieces.

To serve, warm tortillas in pan or microwave to make pliable (Note: this is necessary to keep tortillas from breaking.) The enchiladas can be assembled two ways: 1) how the restaurant does it: Place shrimp on the tortillas, pour red sauce on top, roll and garnish with more salsa and toppings or 2) how I do it: Use tongs to dip the tortillas into the sauce, add shrimp, roll, and garnish.

Tortas Neza

You know you're in good shape when there's a line of people waiting at a to-go window. It's also an excellent indication that an oozy, drippy sandwich will be in your future. (You'll need to sit down and use two hands to eat it.) Manned by Galdino Molinero for the past fourteen years, I'm almost swayed to move closer to Tortas Neza just to devour his sandwiches on a daily basis. Galdino says that naming the tortas after Mexican soccer teams has been one of the keys to his success. Passersby become curious and ask about the team names. Once they hear what the torta contains, they are swayed into ordering it. "Once they've tried them, they love them," he says. But he's way too modest: the specially made torta bread crafted especially for him by a local bakery, along with toppings like sausage, chicken, and egg (and that's on just one torta!) spiked by his own chile de árbol—based hot sauce (which he makes with chile, onion, garlic, and lemon juice) are what keep patrons returning.

TORTAS NEZA
Info: Operates on weekdays out of the to-go window at Juan Bar, 96-15 Roosevelt Ave. Check social media for updates and information.

Getting There: Take the 7 train into Queens to the Junction Blvd. stop.

Tortas Neza's Chicken de Milanesa. *(photo by Andrea Lynn)*

Torta de Milanesa (Mexican-Style Breaded Chicken Cutlet)
Yield: 4 servings

Referred to as "Torta Puebla" at Tortas Neza since they're all named after soccer teams, this puts the breaded and fried Milanesa chicken on a roll. Galdino says he'll make the cutlet for lunch and serve it on a salad with lettuce, tomato, onion, and avocado for another option. Also, he pickles his own jalapeños and preserves his own hot sauce, so you're missing out on that by making it at home. The bread is the most important part, and while it sounds completely unorthodox, I found Portuguese rolls to be the perfect substitute.

FOR THE MILANESA CHICKEN
1 cup panko bread crumbs
2 eggs
2 tablespoons water
Canola oil, as needed
4 chicken cutlets (about 1½ pounds total)
Kosher salt and freshly ground pepper

FOR THE TORTA

4 Mexican breads like bolillos or birote; or Portuguese rolls
Mayonnaise
String cheese, queso fresco, or feta cheese (optional)
1 ½ cups shredded iceberg lettuce
2 to 3 medium tomatoes, sliced
½ red onion, sliced
1 to 2 ripe avocados, sliced
Pickled jalapeños, as needed
Hot sauce (optional)

Make the chicken: Prepare a breading station. In a shallow bowl, add bread crumbs. In another shallow bowl, add eggs and water, whisking together with a fork until frothy.

Add about 1 inch of oil into a large sauté pan, and warm over high heat. Season chicken cutlets with salt and pepper. First, dip both sides of chicken cutlet into the egg mixture and then straight in to the bread crumbs to coat on both sides. Add chicken to the hot oil (if you have a thermometer, you want the oil to be at 350°F). Make sure not to overcrowd the pan. If needed, it's always better to split it up into two batches rather than forcing them all into one pan. Cook until golden brown on both sides, just a couple minutes on each side. Transfer to a paper towel-lined plate.

Make the tortas: Cut each bread piece lengthwise, and spread mayonnaise on both sides. Add the chicken and top with (optional) cheese, lettuce, tomato, onions, avocado, jalapeños, and hot sauce. Either serve the torta as is, or do it the way Galdino does: On a hot griddle or nonstick pan over medium-high heat, add 1 or 2 tortas. Press them down with a spatula (almost like you would a grilled cheese sandwich), and flip over, cooking until they're warm. Repeat with remaining tortas and serve warm.

Rincon Criollo

When Rudy Acosta was rattling off the ingredients in one of Rincon Criollo's mainstay dishes, the forty-five-minute Arroz con Pollo, I halted at his distinction of Budweiser as the beer. "Wait a minute. Can other kinds of beer be used?" I asked, pretty sure the beer was replaceable. Rudy shook his head, repeating that the one-and-only Bud was an essential component. When Rudy took the reins of the decades-old

family-run Rincon Criollo restaurant from his uncle, it came with a very strict rule: "My uncle said, 'Listen, you're in charge now with one condition—you're not touching my menu. You touch my menu, and I'll kill you.'" Right down to the Budweiser beer, Rudy has kept that promise.

The first incarnation of the restaurant was opened in Cuba in 1950 by Rudy's grandfather. A decade later, the restaurant had grown into a two-and-a-half-acre farm with dining, catered events, pony rides for kids—Rudy equates it to a "mini Disneyland" with Rudy's grandfather and his five brothers at the helm. In 1962, the Cuban government began intervening in all businesses, including this one. "They said, you want to stay here, that's great, but you're going to be a manager, not the owner," Rudy says. The family had no choice but to relinquish the business to the government. "It was a very sad time because for twelve years, they were continuing to grow. God knows what would have happened. My grandfather was starting to talk about hotels and stuff like that. This threw a monkey wrench into the whole plan," says Rudy.

It took five years to be able to escape Cuba, and the Acosta brothers moved to New York City, scrimping and saving so the two younger brothers could open the Corona-based Rincon Criollo in 1976. Around five years ago, Rudy transitioned from a career in hotel management to lend a hand in the family business, along with his sister. The restaurant was already incredibly busy, but two years ago, this segued into "crazy busy," thanks to Guy Fieri and the Food Network. "My uncle stayed away from the restaurant for three days [during filming]," says Acosta. "He walked by once, looked in, and kept walking. He didn't want a part of it." Perhaps that was for the best, since Fieri couldn't resist tampering with the menu, suggesting that Acosta add a little of this or that. "I follow the rules that my uncle put together for me. He said, 'You want to come up with something new, do it at your own place, not at my place.' My job here is to keep everything the same, keep the consistency."

The impact of the restaurant's appearance on Fieri's *Diners, Drive-ins and Dives* continues. Every time it re-airs, it reaches 11.5 million people worldwide. "I've got some Mexican employees that told me, 'My family saw me on TV!' Their families in Mexico haven't seen them in five or ten years, but they saw them on the TV recently through the episode. Everybody's crying, everybody's going crazy," he says. Visitors to New York sometimes come straight from the airport, bags in tow. "They don't even wait to go to the hotel and check in."

RINCON CRIOLLO
Info: 40-09 Junction Blvd., Corona; 718-639-8158

See You There: From Manhattan, take the 7 train to the Junction Blvd. stop. Skip a Saturday visit, where the wait can creep to 2½ hours. Mondays are the best bet.

For an authentic experience: Try the Ropa Vieja, 45-minute Arroz con Pollo (versus the quicker version), or the Wednesday oxtail special, Rabo Encendido. Savor a glass of sangria during the meal and save enough room for a dessert of Guava Shells with Cream Cheese.

Arroz con Pollo ████████████████████
Yield: 4 servings ████████████████████

Your spatulas have been warned: Achiote is the turmeric of Cuban and Latin American cuisine. Also, don't make the mistake I did, which is grabbing the straight-up seeds of the annatto tree versus the ground version. Industrial-strength kitchen equipment is needed to grind those seeds, and I ended up with an orange-stained food processor with those full seeds taunting me. This recipe, adapted from Rudy Acosta, is one of the most popular dishes at the restaurant, akin to a Cuban version of paella. "In reality, paella comes from Spain, much like most of our items," Acosta says. "Most of what's called Cuban cuisine is a mixture of your Spanish descent and African." There's a comfort factor to this dish, and in a multiethnic eating experience, I pair it with the Greek salad on page 7.

Arroz con Pollo at Rincon Criollo. *(photo by Janis Turk)*

6 tablespoons extra-virgin olive oil
1 whole chicken, cut into 8 pieces
Kosher salt and freshly ground black pepper, to taste
2 large green bell peppers, finely chopped
     (about 2½ cups)
2 medium yellow onions, finely chopped (about 2½ cups)
6 medium cloves garlic, minced
2 cups long-grained rice
6 to 8 canned whole, peeled tomatoes, quartered
1½ cups white wine
1 (12-ounce) can Budweiser beer
2 cups chicken stock
1½ teaspoons ground cumin powder
1½ teaspoons dried oregano
1½ teaspoons dried basil
1 to 2 tablespoons ground achiote
1 cup frozen peas, thawed
1 cup sliced roasted red peppers

In a large Dutch oven, warm olive oil over medium-high heat.
Generously season chicken pieces with salt and pepper. In two
batches to prevent overcrowding, add chicken pieces, skin side
down, to the oil, and brown on each side, about 8 to 10 minutes

total for each batch. Transfer both chicken batches to a plate, and reserve.

Add bell peppers and onion to the pot, still over medium-high heat. Stirring occasionally, cook the vegetables until tender and softened, about 8 to 10 minutes. Add garlic and rice, cooking about 1 to 2 minutes for garlic to brown. Next, add tomatoes, wine, beer, and chicken stock. Stir to combine, and then add cumin, oregano, basil, 3/4 teaspoon salt, and ½ teaspoon pepper. Add enough achiote powder, about 1 to 2 tablespoons, to get your rice a "rich yellow color," as described by Rudy. Stir the mixture to combine.

Using tongs, place the chicken into one layer on top of the rice (to the best of your ability). Cover the pot with a lid, and reduce heat to low. Let cook until rice is risotto-like—Rudy says the rice should not be allowed to completely dry out; you want a few pools of liquid still at the top—and the chicken is cooked, about 30 to 35 minutes. Remove from heat, stir in peas and roasted red peppers to garnish, and let sit 5 minutes. Taste, adding additional salt and pepper, if needed, and serve.

Reheat Instructions: If you have leftovers, add a few tablespoons of water to the rice when reheating. Yes, the rice gets a bit mushy, but otherwise it will dry out during the reheating process.

Ropa Vieja
Yield: 6 servings

Rudy says people tend to confuse Spanish-inspired food with Mexican food. Cuban food, which is a cross of Spanish and African, doesn't have nearly the spiciness of Mexican. "You're not going to burn your tongue and not be able to feel your mouth," he promises. To make this without a pressure cooker, cook the steak on high for 8 hours in a slow cooker or braise on the stovetop until tender, anywhere from 4 to 6 hours. Cutting up the steak into small pieces also makes it quicker to cook. Recipe adapted from Rodobaldo Acosta.

    3 pounds flank steak
    1 tablespoon vegetable oil
    1 small green bell pepper, seeded and finely chopped
    1 Spanish yellow onion, finely chopped
    2 teaspoons minced garlic
    ⅓ cup white cooking wine

Ropa Vieja at Rincon Criollo. *(photo by Janis Turk)*

1 whole, peeled tomato
1 cup tomato paste
1 cup ketchup
¾ teaspoon ground cumin
½ teaspoon ground white pepper
1 teaspoon ground oregano
1 teaspoon chicken stock base
Kosher salt, to taste
3 cups cooked white rice
2 cups cooked black beans

Add the flank steak to a pressure cooker along with 1 cup water and set it to cook for 45 minutes. (If your pressure cooker has a low and high setting, go for the high.)

About 20 minutes before the steak is finished, add oil to a large pot and warm over medium heat. Add bell pepper and onion, stirring and sautéing until softened, about 6 to 8 minutes. Stir in garlic, and cook for 1 minute. Add wine, tomato, tomato paste, and ketchup, and stir together to combine. Stir in the spices and chicken stock. Bring to a simmer, cover with lid, and cook over low heat.

When meat is done, shred flank steak with forks and/or tongs. Add spoonfuls of beef to the sauce, sprinkling salt on top of each spoonful. Let the meat simmer in the sauce for 20 to 30 minutes. Serve combined with rice and beans.

Tony's Pizzeria & Restaurant

For a no-frills Italian experience, Tony's Pizzeria & Restaurant merits a visit—either the low-key area in the front of the restaurant or the more upscale dining room in the back. Rosa Laucella, who cooks at Tony's, walked me through their lasagna-making process, citing lasagna's popularity as a comfort food.

According to Rosa, the moisture content in the ricotta won't make a difference in lasagna one way or another. So no need to drain the ricotta, like you would if making cannoli at home. Rosa also gave up another cheese secret: "Throw mozzarella into the freezer for 2 to 3 hours and then you grate it. It comes exactly how you see [it] in the grocery store," says Rosa, who also endorses freezing any leftover cheese for future use.

Rosa says when the lasagna is pulled out of the oven, you have to give it time to settle. "The best thing for lasagna is you've got to let it stay; this way all the moisture becomes absorbed. If you try to cut it right away it usually falls all apart. Let it rest half an hour, even an hour if you have time." When reheating, do it the way they do it at the restaurant: Place an individual square in a dish in the oven—the sides get all crispy.

The restaurant's minestrone soup made me wonder why I had never jumped on the minestrone bandwagon. The restaurant's minestrone soup has a little bit of everything, and I mean this in the best possible way. Each bite has a little variation—chickpeas, red beans, lentils, chopped spinach. Rosa explains it originated as a peasant food, meant to use up any ingredients looming in the kitchen or pantry.

TONY'S PIZZERIA & RESTAURANT
Info: 45-18 104th St., Corona; 718-779-1707; tonyspizzerianyc.com

See You There: Take the 7 train into Queens to the 103rd St. stop. Walk east on Roosevelt Ave. and turn right onto 104th St.

Lasagna
Yield: 6 servings

The restaurant adds their homemade marinara sauce to the meat sauce for their lasagna. I shortened the process, just merging both sauces into one. The restaurant also uses equal parts ground beef and ground veal, but if Rosa is preparing at home, she uses a pork/beef/veal combo. "The pork just adds more flavor. Usually you need a little fat in the meat for the meat sauce. If it's too dry, it doesn't have enough fat," she says.

FOR THE TOMATO SAUCE
1 tablespoon canola oil
1 medium onion, finely chopped
5 to 6 celery stalks, finely chopped
4 cloves garlic, minced
½ pound ground veal
½ pound 85 percent lean ground beef
½ cup white wine
1½ (28-ounce) cans crushed tomatoes
1 teaspoon dried oregano
1 teaspoon dried basil
¾ teaspoon kosher salt
¼ teaspoon freshly ground pepper

FOR THE LASAGNA
15 to 20 lasagna noodles
1 (32-ounce) container ricotta
1 (16-ounce) mozzarella ball, shredded or thinly sliced
1 cup grated Parmesan

In a medium, heavy-duty pot, warm canola oil over medium heat. Add onion and celery, sautéing until vegetables have softened, about 10 to 15 minutes, stirring occasionally. Add garlic, stirring to combine and cooking until golden, just 30 seconds to 1 minute. Add ground veal and ground beef, increasing the heat to high. Break meat up with a spatula and sauté until veal is cooked, about 5 minutes. Add wine, cooking until it is reduced and mostly evaporated. Stir in the crushed tomatoes and spices. Bring tomato sauce to a boil, cover, and then reduce heat to low, so the sauce is simmering. Let sauce cook a minimum of 30 minutes. Taste the sauce, adjusting salt and herbs, if necessary.

Preheat oven to 375°F. Cook lasagna noodles in salted water according to package directions until al dente. Drain the noodles in colander. In a 13 x 9-inch pan, spread about 1 cup of tomato sauce on the bottom of the pan. Cover with lasagna noodles and spread 1/3 ricotta over the noodles. Top with 1/3 mozzarella cheese, 1/4 cup Parmesan, and about 2 cups tomato sauce. Repeat for two more layers.

Loosely cover lasagna with foil and place in preheated oven on top of a baking sheet in case of any lasagna spillover. Cook for 30 minutes. Remove foil and top with remaining 1/4 cup Parmesan cheese and cook another 15 minutes. Remove lasagna from oven and let cool for 10 to 15 minutes (otherwise you'll have a soupy, oozy mess). Cut into squares and serve.

A cheesy piece of lasagna from Tony's Pizzeria and Restaurant. (photo by Janis Turk)

Corona Walking Tour

Available for purchase at Citi Field during Mets games, a Mama's sandwich straight from the real  **Ⓐ Leo's Latticini** (46-02 104th St.; 718-898-6069) is a notch better. And I would know; I spent years beelining to their stand in Shea Stadium with my husband before I even knew there was an actual Mama's restaurant. To get there, take the 7 train to 103rd Street—Corona Plaza stop. Walk one block east, make a right on 104th Street, and walk five blocks to Leo's Latticini, which sprawls an entire block with a deli, bakery, and café. Continue on 104th Street and make a left on Corona Avenue and walk 2 blocks. Go to **Ⓑ Cienaga Grocery and Deli** (104-32 Corona Ave.; 347-353-2366) for Oaxacan specialties, including tlayudas, big crisp tortillas with mole and black beans. Continue east down Corona one block, making a slight right onto 108th Street to the half-century-old **Ⓒ The Lemon Ice King of Corona** (52-02 108th St.; 718-699-5133) featured in the opening credits of *The King of Queens* television show. Choose from their selection of sixty Italian ice flavors (peach! rum raisin! pistachio!), like the popularly requested rainbow (cherry, lemon, and blue raspberry) or the raved-about peanut butter ice, all pure-tasting and delightful on the tongue. But be warned: No mixing of flavors is allowed (and many signs around the shop will remind you). Enjoy your ice in adjacent William F. Moore Park and watch the retired men play bocce. Head back west on Corona Avenue about three-quarters of a mile to **Ⓓ Rio de la Plata Bakery Shop** (96-45 Corona Ave.), an Argentinian bakery serving dulce de leche–filled pastries and sandwiches de miga, a recommendation from Queens tour guide Myra Alperson. Walk across the street to the Argentinian butcher **Ⓔ El Gauchito** (94-60 Corona Ave.). Note that El Gauchito is a restaurant/butcher—if there's still room in your stomach, park yourself at a table and split a steak. Otherwise, peruse the meat selection to bring a few cuts of meat home, along with authentic chimichurri sauce. Walk back a half block and make a left on Junction Blvd. Walk nine blocks to Junction Blvd. subway station to catch the 7 train.

QUEENS FOOD PRO: Myra Alperson, owner of Noshwalks Tours and author of *Nosh New York*

What's your Queens claim to food fame? I believe I take people to a greater variety of Queens neighborhoods than any other NYC food tour guide through my Noshwalks Tours. For example, one of my tours includes the Portuguese enclave of Jamaica. Didn't know there was one? There is! I have regular tours to Sunnyside—I don't know of any other food tours that go there— as well as to Ridgewood, Woodside, Richmond Hill's Little Guyana/Little Trinidad and a tour that combines Central Asian Rego Park with Ecuadorean Corona, connected with stops in between that include the Lemon Ice King and Tortilleria Nixtamal. The other destinations of my tours are more typical: Jackson Heights (I have two, one for the Latin American area, the other focusing on South Asian, with increased emphasis on newer destinations offering Nepali and Tibetan food); Flushing; Elmhurst. My tours go to all types of food destinations: restaurants, snack bars, bakeries, food carts, markets.

What's the most surprising food experience you've had in Queens? There isn't one experience I can single out. I always enjoy discovering new foods and places. The only Surinamese place in NYC (to my knowledge) is in Richmond Hill. The only Paraguayan place is in Sunnyside. I believe there's just one kosher Yemeni eatery (Flushing/Kew Garden Hills). The only Chilean eatery/bakery is in Astoria, etc. I love discovering the "onlies," but am always happy to learn there are others. And I feel as though I've just scratched the surface, because the Queens food scene is so dynamic.

Any favorite Queens memories (food-related or not)? Seeing roosters and hens pecking away on the front lawn of a small home belonging to a Salvadoran family in Jamaica, Queens, as if this were an ordinary occurrence in NYC. I haven't seen them in recent years, so the family may have moved away, or they got rid of the birds!

One year I got out of the train at 61st Street and Roosevelt and saw a man selling coffee from a pair of canteens strapped to his back. I'd never seen this before and have to presume this was a tradition exported from South America.

Another year, a group of Noshwalkers were wandering along Roosevelt Ave. in Woodside when a woman at a Korean church beckoned us in. They were serving Korean omelets, which she called "Korean pizza," and they were delicious! I've had similar omelets at other Korean eateries but this was a treat. Queens people are sports fanatics, and it's fun to go into different local eateries and/or bars to watch soccer or cricket or whatever sport the particular neighborhood people are following.

What type of non-food activities do you like to do in Queens or do you recommend others to do?

- Museum of the Moving Image
- Visit fascinating shops tied to the culture of a neighborhood, such as Butala Emporium on 74th Street in Jackson Heights, or Kumari, a Tibetan/Nepali shop on 47th Street in Sunnyside.
- Louis Armstrong House in Corona
- Noguchi Museum
- Rufus King Manor in Jamaica (visit as part of Jamaica, Queens, Noshwalk)

Name something you've only been able to find in a specific Queens location:

- Truly authentic Ecuadorean dishes at El Dorado Café at 102-02 Roosevelt Avenue, which is next door to an excellent Ecuadorean market, Casa America, 102-04 Roosevelt Avenue
- Bakery that makes Uzbek pumpkin dumplings: Rokhat at Austin Avenue
- Certain spices and syrups at Persian Jewish market at Queens Bazaar on 63rd Drive in Rego Park
- Romanian pastries at Nita's European Pastries in Sunnyside
- Tibetan momos at various eateries and food trucks on 37th Road and 74th Street and the immediate surroundings
- Filipino barbecue on Roosevelt Avenue at 69th and 70th streets, including a great place called Ihawan
- Miniature Argentinian pastries, many with dulce de leche, at Confiteria Buenos Aires at 90-09 Roosevelt Avenue
- Uruguayan arrollados at Café Nueva 2000 on 37th Avenue in Jackson Heights

- Chilean hot dogs at San Antonio bakery on Astoria Boulevard around 36th Street
- The amazing grilled octopus at Sabry Restaurant on Steinway Street near Astoria Blvd.

Any specific dishes from Queens restaurants that you've always wanted to make at home? It's much easier to go out and buy them properly made and ready to eat! I once tried to make Salvadoran pupusas and they came out with the consistency of bricks. Some dishes are best left to people who know how to make them right! (Best place to buy pupusas in Queens is El Rincon Salvadoreño in Jamaica.)

What is your favorite . . .

Thai restaurant in Queens: Ayada and Spicy Shallot, both in Elmhurst

Chinese restaurant in Queens: Golden Mall in Flushing, because you feel like you're in a real Chinese village food market with all types of food combinations I've never tried. Although New World Mall is across the street and is very modern and slick, I prefer Golden Mall. Interestingly, Lanzhou Handmade Noodle has stalls in both Golden Mall and New World Mall.

Greek in Queens: Kyclades in Astoria

Mexican in Queens: Tortilleria Nixtamal in Corona

Street cart in Queens: Ecuadorian cart in Sunnyside, 46th Street and Greenpoint Avenue. It's not always there, but I always purchase from them when I see them.

Dessert/bakery in Queens: La Marjolaine in Woodside

Specialty food spot: Morscher's Pork Store in Ridgewood, which is a very old family store. The owners are Slovenian and very friendly! They sell Bauer's Mustard, which is manufactured in Ridgewood. Joe's Pizza at 31st Street and 36th Avenue is Brazilian-owned; they sell salgadinhos, Brazilian finger foods, including delicious codfish cutlets.

Others: Colombian cholados, Colombian baby corn arepas (choclo), El Dorado Café, El Chivito d'Oro—try their Uruguayan arrollados, which are AMAZING, especially those with tuna, olives, and hearts of palm.

The Sunnyside sign welcomes you.
(photo by Andrea Lynn)

SUNNYSIDE

A blast-from-the-past diner-feel at Alpha Donuts. *(photo by Janis Turk)*

SUNNYSIDE

Ranked by *New York* magazine as one of the three most livable neighborhoods in the city, Sunnyside is home to many Colombians, Ecuadorians, Koreans, and Romanians. Perhaps more residential than other areas of Queens without one distinctive ethnic profile, in the last few years the area has really come into its own as far as the restaurant scene. This has been thanks in part to Queens native Daniel Yi, who draws trendy diners to **Salt & Fat**, where he dishes up globally influenced New American small plates, the first of this type of restaurant in the area.

On the ethnic scene, patrons flock to **Natural Tofu Restaurant** to crack eggs into sizzling hot bowls of sundubu, a spicy Korean soup with gobs of fresh tofu. Eastern European immigrants come to **Romanian Garden** for hearty meals of stuffed cabbage, mititei (beef sausage), and donuts smothered in sour cream and jam. And speaking of donuts, the twenty-four-hour diner **Alpha Donuts** nabbed the "Best NYC French Cruller" award by *Serious Eats*; also, make sure to check out the antique cash register, which adds to the old-school feel of this restaurant.

There's also the allure of Sunnyside Gardens, a historic district right next door that is worthy of an extensive stroll through greenery and looming trees, a vision that is hard to believe exists within subway stops of Manhattan.

SALT & FAT

41-16   718-433-3702

Salt & Fat

Homegrown Sunnyside resident Daniel Yi doesn't serve anything at his restaurant that he himself wouldn't want to devour. That's the mantra this chef lives by, forging a menu philosophy that's a cross between the unique foods he wants to eat but made with ingredients that are still familiar to people. "I'm not using crazy ingredients that nobody's ever heard of. All the stuff that I use is very familiar," he says. "We put a little twist on it."

Judging from the mini-gathering that forms on the sidewalk outside of Salt & Fat prior to its 6 p.m. opening, what Yi wants to eat is also popular among others. Salt & Fat takes no reservations, so fans of the Sunnyside restaurant understand the pivotal need for promptness to score a table. This is a far cry from before the restaurant opened; passersby would see the sign and remark on it. "I had a lot of people come by and say, 'You should change your name. Americans are already obese. You're just adding to the problem,'" Yi says. "We do have fatty, rich stuff, but we're making it from scratch. It's not processed. We're using good-quality ingredients. After a while, people started really digging it. They said the name is very catchy and interesting. It went from bad to good."

Yi opened the restaurant almost four years ago after recognizing a void for a progressive restaurant in the Sunnyside area. Then he added in some Asian influences, like those pulled from his Korean-American background. "I grew up on Korean food, but I would go out and eat burgers and pizza with my friends; my mom would try to make spaghetti at home and we would eat it with kimchee on the side." While Yi admits many customers tell him they're thankful for an elevated, ethnic-inspired, small-dish restaurant in Sunnyside, Yi's on the more modest side. "I'm just trying to do good food. That's basically it," he says. What he doesn't mention are the accolades, like *Time Out New York* praising his fried chicken as "some of the best fried fowl we've had in the city" or *The New York Times* declaring dashi-soaked oxtail terrine as "wondrous."

As far as favorite ethnic spots in Queens, Yi has currently been awed by Ongee Crab in Douglaston. "It's basically raw blue crabs. They clean it and pickle it in a soy-based pickle and another one in a spicy chile paste pickle. Basically you just eat it with rice. It's really good," he says. Chao Thai in Elmhurst also gets high marks for Thai food that is reminiscent of time spent in Thailand. "I feel like Queens has the best eats in New York. It's the most diverse and the prices are still friendly," he says. That's why if he opens another restaurant, there's no doubt that it would be in Queens.

SALT & FAT
Info: 41-16 Queens Blvd., Sunnyside; 718-433-3702; saltandfatny.com

See You There: Take the 7 train to Queens to the 40th St. stop. Walk east to Queens Blvd. to 41st St.

What's Popular: Yi says the two mainstays on the menu since opening have been the Scallops with Roasted Carrot Purée and the Oxtail Terrine. The Crispy Pork Trotter and Fried Chicken are also favorites.

Sea Scallops with Truffled Corn Salsa and Roasted Carrot Purée
Yield: 4 servings

Daniel Yi thinks the key to this dish's success is that it's well-balanced: "You take a bite of the sweet carrot purée with the corn salsa, which is acidic, and the fried capers, which are salty, so you've got sweet, acid, salty all in one bite." Caramelizing the carrots enhance their sweetness, and Daniel advises buying the "best scallops you can get." For the sake of making this recipe a little easier (and dirtying fewer sauté pans), I incorporated the capers into the salsa versus frying them. Also, I've adapted this Daniel Yi recipe into an entrée-size portion.

FOR THE CARROT PURÉE
1½ pounds medium-sized carrots, washed and
    trimmed of greens
1 tablespoon olive oil
Kosher salt and freshly ground pepper
½ cup heavy cream
3 tablespoons butter, cut into pieces
2½ tablespoons maple syrup

FOR THE SCALLOPS AND TRUFFLE-CORN SALSA

½ tablespoon extra-virgin olive oil

3 pieces corn on the cob, shucked and cut off the cob
  (about 2½ to 3 cups corn kernels)

1½ tablespoons finely minced shallots

¼ cup chopped chives

1 tablespoon capers, rinsed and chopped

1 tablespoon rice wine vinegar

3 tablespoons truffle oil

Kosher salt and freshly ground pepper

2 tablespoons canola oil, plus more if needed

2 pounds sea scallops, rinsed and patted dry
  with paper towels

Start the carrot purée: Preheat oven to 450°F. Add whole carrots to a large, foil-lined baking sheet, drizzling them with olive oil, salt, and pepper. Cook carrots in the oven until tender and caramelized, about 1 hour. (The length of time will depend on the thickness of the carrots, so the time could vary from 30 minutes to 1 hour.) Add cream, butter, maple syrup, salt, and pepper into the bowl of a food processor along with the carrots. Let the steam from the carrots melt the butter for about 1 minute; purée until mixture is smooth, adding a bit more heavy cream for a thinner consistency, if needed. Taste, adjusting seasonings if needed. Cover to keep warm.

Make the salsa: Meanwhile, in a large sauté pan, warm olive oil over medium-high heat. Add corn, and sauté until bright yellow and cooked, about 3 to 5 minutes. Transfer to a container, and let corn cool, even placing in the freezer for a bit to chill.

To serve, add corn to a bowl along with shallots, chives, capers, vinegar, truffle oil, salt, and pepper. Taste, adjusting vinegar, truffle oil, salt, and pepper if needed.

In a large sauté pan over high heat, warm canola oil. Season the scallops with salt and pepper. Add scallops to the pan, but avoid overcrowding. (Overcrowding will make the scallops steam versus sauté, and you won't get a crust on them.) Cook about 2 to 3 minutes on one side, until the bottom is browned. Flip over with a spatula and cook about 1 more minute. You want the scallops to still be translucent in the center, which is the telltale sign that they're perfectly cooked. To serve, add carrot purée to each plate, top with scallops, and divide corn salsa between each plate over the scallops.

Korean Barbecue Lettuce Wraps with Marinated Steak and Pickled Vegetables

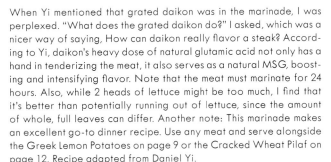

Yield: 4 servings

When Yi mentioned that grated daikon was in the marinade, I was perplexed. "What does the grated daikon do?" I asked, which was a nicer way of saying, How can daikon really flavor a steak? According to Yi, daikon's heavy dose of natural glutamic acid not only has a hand in tenderizing the meat, it also serves as a natural MSG, boosting and intensifying flavor. Note that the meat must marinate for 24 hours. Also, while 2 heads of lettuce might be too much, I find that it's better than potentially running out of lettuce, since the amount of whole, full leaves can differ. Another note: This marinade makes an excellent go-to dinner recipe. Use any meat and serve alongside the Greek Lemon Potatoes on page 9 or the Cracked Wheat Pilaf on page 12. Recipe adapted from Daniel Yi.

FOR THE MEAT
²/₃ cup soy sauce
3 tablespoons honey
¹/₃ cup sesame oil
1 cup grated daikon (about 1 medium daikon)
2 jalapeños, chopped
4 garlic cloves, minced
2 pounds skirt steak, cut into equal-sized pieces (or 2 pounds boneless, skinless chicken thighs)

FOR THE WRAPS
1 cup sugar
1 ½ cups white vinegar
2 ½ cups water
2 large daikons, thinly sliced
4 jalapeños, thinly sliced
2 medium heads Boston or Bibb lettuce leaves
1 small red onion, sliced, to serve

FOR THE SHALLOTS
8 shallots
Canola oil, as needed

To marinate the meat: In a large ziplock bag, add soy sauce, honey, sesame oil, grated daikon, chopped jalapeños, and minced garlic. Use a spoon to combine the mixture together. Add skirt steak, seal the plastic bag, and refrigerate for about 24 hours.

To make the quick-pickled vegetables: Add sugar, vinegar, and water in a medium pot. Bring to a boil over high heat, and stir until sugar is dissolved. Remove from heat, and add daikon and jalapeño slices. Transfer to a container and refrigerate for about 24 hours.

When ready to serve, make the shallots: Peel and thinly slice the shallots. Using a heavy-duty medium pot fitted with a thermometer, add a couple inches of canola oil and warm over high heat to around 325° to 350°F. Add ⅓ of the shallots, cooking until very golden, about 2 to 3 minutes. Use a slotted spoon to transfer fried shallots to a paper towel-lined plate. Continue until all the shallots are fried.

Meanwhile, remove the leaves from lettuce head. Wash and dry in a salad spinner. Warm a large nonstick pan over high heat. Add the steak pieces, making sure not to overcrowd the pan (cooking in batches, if necessary). Cook the steak to desired doneness, about 2 to 3 minutes per side for medium-rare. Transfer steak to a plate, cover with foil, and let rest about 5 minutes. (If using chicken instead of steak, cook about 5 minutes per side until internal temperature reaches 165°F.)

Thinly slice the red onion. Add onions, pickled jalapeños and pickled daikon to a platter, along with lettuce leaves. Cut the steak on the bias. Top lettuce leaves with steak and vegetables, garnishing with fried shallots.

FOOD SHOP: Butcher Block

Irish food tends to get a bad rap, including by me—I'm still haunted by a trip to Ireland filled with plates of overcooked salmon and underseasoned boiled potatoes. My one shining memory of the country is their Irish breakfasts, which can be re-created with a visit to Butcher Block. And that was just the reason Irish-raised co-owner Noel Gaynor opened the establishment almost two decades ago: to give Irish expats access to their homeland's butchery goods, like Irish bacon and blood sausage (also known as black pudding). The sausages are done Italian-style, says Noel, with the meat ground twice for a smoother texture.
What was first a small aisle of Irish goods swelled to overtake a vast majority of the store because of their popularity. There's Irish newspapers, soda bread flown in from Ireland, and top sellers like the digestive cookies and tea selection. Also, make sure to browse through the expansive British selections, such as jams (even Jameson whiskey marmalade), sodas, chocolates, and crisps in flavors like prawn and pickled onion.

For your own Irish breakfast, go straight to the back of the store for a prepackaged Irish breakfast. Gaynor assures that it's the same as the one from the butcher counter, just assembled ahead of time and meant for two. There's Irish bacon, which is the same cut as a boneless pork chop that is cured, making it considerably less fatty than America's bacon counterpart (and Gaynor advises to sauté it in a bit of oil). Black pudding, white pudding, and Irish sausage are also a part of the Irish breakfast package; while I always thought sautéed tomato slices were an essential part of the breakfast, Gaynor says no. (I say it certainly doesn't hurt!)

An array of jams at Butcher Block. *(photo by Andrea Lynn)*

BUTCHER BLOCK
Info: 43-46 41st St; 718-784-1078

See You There: Take the 7 train to the 40th St. stop.

Shepherd's Pie
Yield: 4 servings

Noel Gaynor says not to ruin an Irish Shepherd's Pie with herbs and seasonings, but rather to embrace it for what it is. He uses beef in his Butcher Block version but says beef or lamb will do. Also, the way it's dished out at Butcher Block is rather ingenious to a Shepherd's Pie lover like myself. The veggies are mixed in with the meat and gravy; then it's topped with spoonfuls of mashed potatoes (instead of layered in a casserole form) and a hefty portion of even more gravy is poured on top. Recipe adapted from Butcher Block.

FOR THE MASHED POTATOES
2 pounds potatoes, such as Russet, peeled and cubed
3 tablespoons unsalted butter, thinly sliced
¾ cup milk (preferably whole milk)
½ teaspoon kosher salt
½ teaspoon freshly ground pepper

FOR THE MEAT
1 tablespoon olive oil
1 onion, finely chopped
2 cups chopped carrots (about 4 to 5 medium carrots)
1 pound lean (85 percent) ground beef or
   ground lamb
Salt and freshly ground pepper
1 (10-ounce) bag frozen peas, thawed
1 tablespoon butter
2½ tablespoons all-purpose flour
2 (10½-ounce) cans beef consommé

Make the mashed potatoes: In a large pot over high heat, add potatoes and enough water to cover. Add salt, and bring to a boil, cooking until fork-tender, about 12 minutes. Drain potatoes, and transfer to a large bowl. Add butter, stirring to melt. Add ½ cup milk, salt, and pepper mixture into potatoes and mash with a potato masher until the mixture is smooth. For a creamier consistency, add additional milk.

Make the meat: Preheat oven to 400°F. While potatoes cook, preheat a large skillet over medium-high heat. Warm the oil in the pan, and sauté onions and carrots until soft, about 6 minutes. Add ground meat, salt, and pepper. Sauté the meat, breaking up the meat with a fork, for 3 or 4 minutes. Add peas, and cook a couple minutes until warm. Using a slotted spoon, transfer meat mixture to an 8 x 8-inch baking dish, leaving about 1 tablespoon of fat in the pan (If there isn't enough fat, just add the amount in canola oil).

Over medium-high heat in the same skillet pan, add butter and flour to beef fat to form a roux. Add consommé and whisk constantly for 5 to 6 minutes to thicken gravy. When desired thickness is achieved, remove from heat. Taste the gravy, adjusting seasonings if needed. Pour half the gravy into the reserved meat mixture, and stir to combine. Use a spatula to make into one even layer. Top with a layer of potatoes, and then spoon additional gravy on top (make tiny craters into the mashed potatoes to better hold the gravy). Cook in the preheated oven until warm, about 10 to 15 minutes.

Romanian Garden

Throughout our meals at Romanian Garden, my husband kept pointing out, perplexed, that the crowd seemed to be all Romanian. But it's a perfect neighborhood restaurant, he kept saying, citing that it was affordable with hearty portions of good food and a family friendly environment. I should mention that my husband doesn't get cranky when he's hungry, unlike myself. Prepare to wait a good twenty to thirty minutes just for a glass of water, let alone ordering your meal. Knowing you are embarking on a leisurely meal experience throughout Eastern Europe

The heavenly sour cream-drenched donuts (papanasi) at Romanian Garden. *(photo by Andrea Lynn)*

can make all the difference between enjoying the restaurant...or not. The waitstaff is evenly divided between helpful and curt employees. Upon a recommendation from *Gourmet Live*, I ventured for the tripe version of Romanian sour soup, a light yet dairy-swirled soup with the softest, most delicious tripe I've ever experienced. And I'm not one to use "delicious" and "tripe" in the same sentence often. A whole jalapeño comes on the side, and I wish someone had told me exactly what I was supposed to do with it (chomp on it as I sipped the soup?). It's all Romanian comfort food, like the eggplant salad and fried zucchini served with vinegar for sprinkling and a potent garlic purée for dipping. More salty and garlicky, the skinless Romanian beef sausages are served with tomato-based white beans heightened with dill, almost like an Eastern European play on America's baked beans. The fried donuts topped with jam and a pillowy white sauce of thinned sour cream is an absolute must. So much a must, that if you're in the neighborhood, it's worth a stop just to try them.

ROMANIAN GARDEN
Info: 43-06 43rd Ave., Sunnyside; 718-786-7894

See You There: Take the 7 train to Queens to the 46th Street stop; walk north on 46th St. toward 43rd Ave. and make a left onto it.

For an Authentic Experience: Order the Ciorba De Burta Tripe Soup, Dovlecei pane (fried zucchini with garlic), Mamaliga Cu Brinza Si Smintina (cheesy polenta), Mititei (skinless Romanian sausages), and, of course, the Papanasi (donuts topped with jam and a sour cream sauce).

Papanasi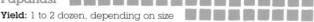

Yield: 1 to 2 dozen, depending on size

Romanian Garden wasn't exactly forthcoming on any of the happenings inside their kitchen. One of the problems is that the restaurant is constantly packed. Even during the afternoon lull experienced by many other restaurants, their dining room was filled with Romanians watching European sports and drinking beer. Since I couldn't get the papanasi out of my mind, I took it upon myself to figure out how to make them. Recipe inspired by Romanian Garden.

1 (16-ounce) container 1 percent low-fat cottage cheese
2 eggs
¼ cup granulated sugar
1 cup all-purpose flour
½ teaspoon baking soda
Canola oil, for frying
Apricot, raspberry, or cherry jam or preserves
1 (8-ounce) container sour cream
¼ cup water

In a large bowl, add cheese, eggs, sugar, flour, and baking soda. Gently mix to combine. Place in the refrigerator and let mixture sit for at least 1 hour.

In a heavy-duty medium pot, add enough canola oil to fill it at least halfway. Fasten a thermometer onto the pan and bring to 325°F over high heat. (If you don't have a thermometer, sprinkle a dusting of flour over the oil—if it sizzles, the oil is ready to go.) Fill a small spoon with dough mixture and use another spoon to push it into the hot oil, cooking just a few at a time. Let doughnuts cook until puffy and golden, just a few minutes. (As you continue to cook, the oil will need to be tinkered with, lowering to medium-high if the donuts cook too quickly.) Use a slotted spoon, remove and transfer to a paper towel-lined plate. Repeat until all the donuts have been fried.

In a small bowl, add sour cream and thin out with water, using a spoon to combine. To serve, plate the donuts, spoon sour cream mixture over them, and add about a spoonful of jam or preserves on top.

Natural Tofu Restaurant

Homemade, melt-in-your-mouth soft tofu is a revelation to those who may only have experienced grocery store tofu. Floating in the spicy, beef-broth-based Korean stew of sundubu in the low-thrills environment of Natural Tofu serves as a warm-up for a winter's day.

A spread arrives during the sundubu wait: little dishes of bean sprouts, cucumber kimchee, cabbage kimchee, fish cakes, and a raw egg to crack and cook when the boiling hot stew comes to the table. There's also a little bowl of pinkish, slightly tart cold soup. I remember being perplexed when it was first served: Was this an appetizer or to sip with the soup? On a return visit, manager Ranjit Hirachan explained that it's meant to drink alongside the soup, as a cool-down method. The tofu soup comes with a bowl of stickyish rice. Hirachan says there's no right or wrong way to eat it—it's all about preference: "Some eat a bit of rice, then the soup. Some mix it together." The sundubu is the main draw at the restaurant, available in seven varieties like kimchee, seafood, beef, and even beef intestine in a spice range of mild (just half a spoonful of Korean pepper paste added in the kitchen) to very spicy (about 1½ spoonfuls). Order the Korean barbecue-marinated LA Galbi, thinly sliced bone-in short ribs marinated and basted in a top-secret Korean barbecue sauce to split along with the soup.

NATURAL TOFU RESTAURANT
Info: 40-06 Queens Blvd., Sunnyside; 718-706-0899

See You There: Take the 7 train to Queens to the 40th St. stop; walk east on Queens Blvd. to the restaurant.

For an Authentic Experience: Split the Kimchee Pancakes, your choice of one of the Sundubu dishes, and the LA Golbi.

One of five vats of sundubu at Natural Tofu.
(photo by Janis Turk)

Korean-Style Kimchee Pancakes ■■■■■■■■
Yield: 4 appetizer servings ■■■■■■■■■■■■■

At Natural Tofu, a large kimchee pancake sliced into pizzalike wedges is served. For ease, I've made small pancakes that are less cumbersome to turn during cooking. Never pour out a pancake that is too big to flip, otherwise it'll break midflip. Also, rice flour incorporated into the pancake adds a crispier texture versus using just all-purpose flour. Add ¼ cup cooked ground pork for another tasty element. Recipe inspired by Natural Tofu Restaurant.

FOR THE KIMCHEE PANCAKE
¾ cup all-purpose flour
¼ cup rice flour
2 large eggs
½ cup water
¼ cup kimchee juice (from kimchee jar)
1 cup chopped kimchee
2 scallions, chopped
1 jalapeño, finely chopped
¼ teaspoon kosher salt
Canola oil, as needed

FOR THE DIPPING SAUCE
¼ cup soy sauce
3 tablespoons rice vinegar
1 scallion, finely chopped
Sriracha, as needed (optional)

In a medium bowl, add flours, egg, water, and kimchee juice. Combine until just mixed (no more), and let batter sit for 15 to 20 minutes. Meanwhile, in a small bowl, combine the dipping sauce ingredients, tasting and adjusting ingredients if necessary.

After the batter has sit, stir in kimchee, scallions, jalapeño, and salt. Lightly cover the bottom of a small 6- or 8-inch nonstick pan (an omelet pan works perfectly) with oil, and warm over medium-high heat. Add enough batter to coat about three-fourths of the pan; cook until bottom is golden, just 2 to 4 minutes. Use a spatula to flip, and cook until that side is golden, about 2 to 3 minutes. Remove, transfer to a paper towel-lined plate, and coat the pan with more oil, if needed. Repeat until the batter is done, usually about 2 to 3 more pancakes. Pancakes are best served piping hot with dipping sauce.

LA Galbi at Natural Tofu. *(photo by Janis Turk)*

LA Galbi

Yield: 4 to 6 servings

The most difficult part of this recipe is tracking down the thinly cut short ribs. If your butcher won't cut bone-in short ribs for you (ask for them to be cut about ½-inch thick and across the bone), consider just using boneless short ribs. All the ingredients can be added to a crockpot and cooked on low for 8 hours for a Korean-inspired short rib dish. Serve with sticky rice and a side of kimchee. Recipe inspired by Natural Tofu Restaurant.

½ cup soy sauce
¼ cup sesame oil
¼ cup Shaoxin cooking wine or sherry
¼ cup dark molasses or dark brown sugar
3 cloves garlic
1 (2-inch) piece gingerroot, peeled and cut into pieces
2 scallions
1 Asian pear, slices into pieces*
3 pounds LA Galbi (thinly cut, bone-in short ribs)

In the bowl of a food processor, add soy sauce, sesame oil, wine or sherry, molasses, garlic, ginger, scallions, and pear. Pulse until mixture is puréed, around 1 minute. Add LA Galbi to a ziplock bag and cover with marinade. Seal the plastic bag, and refrigerate for 12 to 24 hours.

When ready to serve, preheat the broiler to a high setting. Remove the ribs from the marinade, blotting the marinade from the meat with paper towels. Place on a foil-lined baking sheet, and cook under a broiler until charred, about 5 to 6 minutes just on one side. Remove from broiler, using kitchen shears to cut each rib at the bone into pieces.

* **Substitution:** 1 firm, barely-ripe pear can be subbed for the Asian pear.

QUEENS FOOD PRO: Max Falkowitz, *Serious Eats* editor

What made you move to Queens and how long have you lived here? I grew up in Forest Hills, and other than a stint at college, I haven't lived anywhere but Queens. The question was never, "Where do I go next?" It was all always, "When can I get back?"

Name the reasons you love Queens: The people, who are incredibly down-to-earth but capable of schooling you in everything if you pause to listen. The food, which is, of course, endlessly fascinating. The diversity—I just don't feel comfortable living somewhere that doesn't have people from everywhere, and no place does that better than Queens.

New York is changing, and a lot of people are getting worried about whether its most precious elements—its neurotic strangeness, its endless diversity, the rush of immigrants and dreamers working to find a place for themselves—are getting priced out of town. I don't know how bad the problem is. But I do believe that Queens is a vanguard of everything we hold dear about this city.

What's your Queens claim to food fame? There are so many reporters with better, more comprehensive, and more in-depth knowledge of the food scene here. But I think I've been successful in highlighting certain businesses that draw people across the East River—and keep them coming back for more. Some of them are new, others are institutions I grew up with. Really, it's all about showing off my hometown to anyone who'll listen.

What do you think is the biggest misconception about Queens (food-related or not)? That it's all "weird" food, not something to eat "when you're just looking for a normal place to eat." I hate when people ask me that. What, you think everyone in this restaurant is here for a weird night out? It also bugs me—though perhaps I should be grateful, as this deters many from moving here and raising my rent—that Queens is perceived as some far-off place slightly less remote from the city than Staten Island. If I ride my bike for half an hour I'm in Williamsburg. And I don't bike that fast!

What's the most surprising experience (foodwise) you've had in Queens? I remember the first time I went to the Ganesh Temple Canteen in Flushing. I first heard about it from an Indian friend on Long Island whose family would drive over for regular meals. I had no idea that part of Flushing even had an Indian population, let alone one large enough to sustain a massive, beautiful temple with a huge food section. Then I tasted a dosa there—a ridiculously simple pancake made from fermented rice and lentils with unconscionable amounts of butter—and it was the best dosa I'd ever tasted. ...From a place that I didn't know existed a week before. And it was in the basement of some temple in the suburbs. That's when it first really hit me that Queens has an endless supply of amazing things.

I was reminded of this when I visited Fang Gourmet Tea, also in Flushing, which is a world-class tea shop selling incredible Taiwanese teas. It's in a mall. A tasting costs $3 for tea that can cost as much as $600 a pound retail. That shop is a gift to New York.

Any favorite Queens memories? I remember my first Greek Easter in Astoria. I woke up around midnight to the sound of clanging church bells and a dirge of voices chanting endlessly. It felt like it was coming from everywhere, and for a moment I really thought the world was going to end. Then I looked at the calendar and did the math. "Oh, it's just midnight mass for Greek Easter." Goodnight.

Describe your ideal eating day in Queens: This is a horribly unfair question. But I'll say that a day without dumplings from Flushing is a day not fully lived.

Are there a string of restaurants that you constantly recommend to others and, if so, what are they? The Ganesh temple, dumplings from Tianjin Dumpling House, mezze at Telly's Taverna and Grill 43, street meat and falafel from the King of Falafel and Shawarma, steak from El Gauchito, ice cream from Eddie's Sweet Shop. But that's just the beginning.

Name something you've only been able to find in a specific Queens location:
The best dumplings are in Flushing, particularly one type made with lamb at Tianjin Dumpling House in the Golden Shopping Mall. The tea at Fang Gourmet in Flushing is like nothing else. The gyros at BZ Grill are incomparable. The suadero at Los Portales in Astoria are gorgeous.

What are a few under-the-radar food places in Queens? I wish more people paid attention to our Lebanese and Turkish restaurants. Wafa's, Souk El Shater, Grill 43, and Cedars all deserve more respect than they get. I think they're all more accomplished than the more celebrated Egyptian places on Steinway.

Any Queens restaurant, food shop, truck, etc. that closed down for which you're still in mourning? Mundo in Astoria served a curious but wonderful mix of Turkish and Argentinian food, most of it vegetarian, all of it thoughtful and delicious. The owners had a great success on their hands but got bored with the stationary brick and mortar, so they sold the business to friends. I still miss their carrot dip and red lentil patties.

Any specific dishes from Queens restaurants that you've always wanted to make at home? If I could make beans like they do at Telly's, shawarma like the King of Falafel's, and menemen like they do at Grill 43, I'm pretty sure I'd never need to cook anything else again.

What is your favorite...

Italian restaurant in Queens: I don't have a standout place, but I enjoy Park Side, a thirty-year-old red sauce joint, which is as old school as it gets.

Thai restaurant in Queens: Ayada and Chao Thai, but I think there's some room for growth in this field.

Chinese restaurant in Queens: Fu Run is probably the restaurant I frequent most often, but my favorite Chinese comes from specialists in food courts that do a couple of things brilliantly.

Pizza in Queens: This is more Brooklyn's domain, but Nick's in Forest Hills has always treated me well.

Dim sum in Queens: I think Chinatown has us beat here, but East Ocean Palace does dim sum as good as I've had in Manhattan.

Greek in Queens: Most of the Greek places here are more similar than different, and I don't think you'll find much consensus about the best. I'm a fan of Telly's Taverna, Gregory's 26, and MP Taverna.

Mexican in Queens: Still seeking transcendental Mexican, but I have a lot of respect for Casa Enrique, which is a more modern, refined take on the cuisine that doesn't compromise what matters.

Street cart in Queens: Freddy, the king of falafel and shawarma, makes the best street food I've had in the city. The man knows his falafel, and his chicken and lamb with tahini, hot sauce, and pickled turnips are some kind of magic.

Dessert/bakery in Queens: Queens is seriously lacking in great bakeries, but Artopolis, Cannelle Patisserie, and La Boulangerie are my favorites.

Specialty food spot: I have a hard time walking into Titan Foods without walking out at least thirty dollars poorer.

Korean-style Kimchee Pancakes at Natural Tofu. *(photo by Janis Turk)*

One of many meat options available at Ottomanelli & Sons Prime Meat Shop. *(photo by Andrea Lynn)*

Fried fish for snacking at Phil-Am Food Mart. *(photo by Andrea Lynn)*

WOODSIDE

In the 1800s, Woodside boasted the largest Irish community in Queens. Traditional Irish fare, like shepherd's pie and fish & chips, can still be found at pubs like **Donovan's Pub**. Burger aficionados have spent years flocking to the restaurant for its famous burger, although less so in recent years due to ownership changes. While in Woodside, roam the area where 61st Street, Roosevelt Avenue, and Woodside Avenue converge to grab soda bread and Irish butter from the many Irish delis and bakeries.

Although Woodside is known for its Irish heritage, it also has a large Asian population. The area is home to **SriPraPhai**, what many consider the best Thai restaurant in NYC. Started more than twenty years ago by Thai-born Sripraphai Tipmanee, locals kept it a secret for years until *Chowhound* forums exploded with its discovery, prompting a praise-filled **New York Times** review that changed everything. Foodies took the 7 train and descended onto the restaurant, which had to expand its seating to accommodate the crowds. Popular menu selections include watercress salad, minced pork with chiles, and beef panang.

Korean restaurant **Sik Gaek** offers another dose of Asian fare with octopus and short rib hot pots, and barbecue pits at every table. Adventurous eaters, like Anthony Bourdain and Momofuku's David Chang, flock to Sik Gaek for a taste of the live young octopus, which arrives at the table still wiggling. If consuming live sea creatures isn't your thing, don't worry. There's still plenty of other menu items to choose from, like the seafood pancakes, bibimbap, and barbecued meat, but keep in mind that the large-portioned menu is skewed for a table of four or more people.

SriPraPhai 899-9599 SriPraPhai

(photo by Andrea Lynn)

Filipinos are a significant group in the neighborhood. "Little Manila" stretches from 63rd Street to 71st Street with restaurants serving up authentic Filipino barbecue, avocado soup, and sizzling sisig (marinated meat). For a sweet treat, walk over to **Red Ribbon,** a fast-food bakery with over two hundred locations in the Philippines and one in New York. The menu features halo-halo, mocha mamon (sponge cake), and the mango delight. Then there's the Filipino grocery store treasure **Phil-Am Food Mart** to pick up traditional favorites, like spicy longaniza sausages, pork lumpia, and pancit noodles.

If you're not in the mood for Asian food, the taco trucks on Roosevelt Avenue show up around 8 p.m. and are known to be among the best food trucks in all of New York City. Two-dollar tacos (topped with cilantro and other goodies) and a one-dollar bottle of apple soda will keep your stomach happy.

SriPraPhai

One of my first eye-opening experiences at SriPraPhai was an afternoon adventure at the restaurant with a food writer with Thai experience who guided me on what to order. Sure, I had been to SriPraPhai before, but was easily overwhelmed by the seemingly never-ending menu (currently at more than 120 items). So I'd regress, order Pad Thai (one of their popular entrées), and call it a day. The menu is intimidatingly expansive, but not if you're armed with pointers to narrow down the choices.

SriPraPhai began almost a quarter of a century ago when namesake Sripraphai Tipmanee opened a storefront in Jackson Heights showcasing her cake-baking and decorating talents. The bakery was less-than-thriving due to the location, except for loyal Thai customers who would order cakes and relish the few simple Thai dishes Sripraphai had added to the selection. Soon, she relocated to a small building in Woodside, realizing her success could lie in giving customers a taste of Thailand. Her son, Lersak, says that Thai customers began telling their friends, which swelled into a mostly Asian-based flock of restaurant-goers.

A decade ago, it was serendipitous when the buildings on both sides of their location went up for sale, creating a chance to expand.

Sripraphai had already made the decision to buy one of the buildings, then took a leap of faith in purchasing both. "My mother called me and said, 'I'm sure we have enough business.'" That's when Lersak's path changed; with an MBA in finance, he quit his career in the Thai banking industry and moved his family to the New York City area.

Sripraphai's hunch was correct. Soon *The New York Times'* Frank Bruni and the *Village Voice* singled out their Thai food, bringing a new clientele not just to the restaurant but also to Queens. On weekends, you'll find all of their 154 seats—plus the 80 seats in the outdoor patio in warmer months—full. Battered and fried watercress salad tossed with coconut flakes, among a plethora of other Thai ingredients, is a popular selling point, as is the soft-shell crab selection, which Lersak says is especially popular among Filipinos. Both these items are among Lersak's favorites, too, and he cites the heightened-flavor and plentiful meat from the Thai-imported crabs as one reason for their success. It's also the infusion of kaffir lime leaves (not an easy ingredient to score) to their curries and other dishes that Lersak thinks make the difference. "It has a lot of flavor, and Thai food really cannot live without kaffir lime leaves," he says, adding that 180 pounds of them are used annually.

The restaurant has also stayed current, adding icons to alert customers with dietary restrictions if items have gluten, fish sauce, and more. And Sripraphai's mom remains a daily fixture at the Woodside location, even living upstairs from the restaurant, while Lersak is closer to the Long Island location. "She's very proud because she is the main person that brings it to this point," he says. "She's at the restaurant all the time."

SRIPRAPHAI

Info: 64-13 39th Ave., Woodside; 718-899-9599; sripraphairestaurant.com

See You There: Take the 7 into Queens to the 69th St. stop. Exit at Roosevelt Ave. and head west toward 68th St. Make a right on 39th Ave. and you practically run into the restaurant. Be warned that it is closed on Wednesdays and incredibly busy on weekend nights.

For an Authentic Experience: Get the Crispy Chinese Watercress Salad or Papaya Salad as an appetizer; Tom-Yum Shrimp Soup or Jumbo Noodle Soup (with pig offal and egg); and split a noodle dish like Pad Thai or Drunken Noodles, along with one of the Soft-shell Crab or Fried Fish (especially the Whole Striped Bass) options.

Drunken Noodles

Makes 4 to 6 servings

Lersak Tipmanee says their Drunken Noodles is a simpler dish to prepare at home, mainly because it requires fewer ingredients than most of their main dishes. "The flat noodle you can buy from the market or, you can use the dry noodle and soak in the water and use. But fresh flat noodle would probably be the best," he says. If using dried noodles, after soaking, use your fingers to make sure noodles haven't stuck together, so sauce can adhere to them. Golden Mountain Sauce, available at Asian stores and through online retailers, is made from fermented soybeans but with a touch of sweetness that makes it a mainstay in numerous Thai dishes. If unable to find, just increase the amount of soy sauce by 2 tablespoons. Recipe adapted from Lersak Tipmanee.

> 1 (16-ounce) package wide flat rice noodles
> 2 tablespoons canola oil
> 2 cups basil leaves, divided
> 4 cloves garlic, chopped
> 3 tablespoons chopped Thai chiles (about 12 to 15 Thai chiles)
> 2 red bell peppers, sliced
> 1 pound ground chicken
> ¼ cup fish sauce
> ¼ cup soy sauce
> ¼ cup Golden Mountain Sauce
> 1 tablespoon honey

Prepare the rice noodles according to the package instructions. Reserve.

In a large sauté pan, warm oil over high heat. Add 1½ cups basil leaves, stirring and cooking until wilted, just 1 or 2 minutes. Add garlic, chiles, and sliced red bell peppers, cooking just 30 seconds. Add chicken, stirring to break up the meat and sautéing until cooked, about 4 to 5 minutes.

Meanwhile, in a small bowl, combine fish sauce, soy sauce, Golden Mountain Sauce and honey. When chicken is cooked, add the combined sauce along with noodles. Using tongs, combine noodles with meat and sauce until noodles are soft and brown, having soaked up all the liquid sauce, about 4 to 5 minutes. Garnish with remaining basil.

SriPraPhai's Shredded Green Mango Salad.
(photo by Andrea Lynn)

Shredded Green Mango Salad ■ ■ ■ ■ ■ ■ ■ ■ ■

While SriPraPhai gets green mangos straight from Florida, it's not as easy to acquire these unripened mangos in the United States if you're not in the food business. Usually found at Asian grocery stores in Queens, I've also had success finding them at Patel Brothers in Jackson Heights. If you're able to pounce on a green papaya versus a green mango (which somehow was easier to find in the area where I live), just go with it—the fruits have a similar taste profile when unripe. (Use about 2 to 3 medium green papayas or about 6 green mangos for this recipe.) Or just pick the greenest, firmest mangos in your produce aisle. Also, SriPraPhai incorporates chicken and calamari into this dish; I've left those out for the sake of ease (isn't it enough that you'll be running around looking for green mangos?). If you want to add chicken, just sauté about ½ pound chicken breasts, thinly slice, and chill until ready for the salad. Another option is to bulk it up with ½ pound cooked and thinly sliced shrimp. While most recipes advise to eat this salad promptly, I like letting it sit for about 30 minutes so it can absorb flavors. Recipe adapted from Lersak Tipmanee.

> 8 cups shredded green mango or green papaya
> ¼ cup freshly squeezed lime juice
> ¼ cup fish sauce
> 3 tablespoons palm sugar or honey
> 5 to 6 Thai chiles (depending on desired heat level),
>   finely chopped
> 1 tablespoon small dried shrimp or 2 teaspoons
>   fermented shrimp paste*
> 1 clove garlic
> 3 tablespoons crushed peanuts
> 4 scallions, chopped
> ⅓ cup halved cashews
> ½ cup chopped cilantro, divided

Peel the skin of the mango or papaya, and remove the seed/seeds. Julienne the fruit, either by using a mandoline or a food processor with julienne attachment. Add into a large bowl.

In the bowl of a food processor, add lime juice, fish sauce, palm sugar, chiles, dried shrimp, garlic, and peanuts. Purée until mixture is liquefied, about 1 minute. Taste, adjusting any of the components if needed. You want a delicate balance of sour, salty, sweet, spicy, and fishy. Transfer mixture to a large bowl.

Stir the mango or papaya shreds into the sauce, along with scallions, nuts, and ¼ cup cilantro. Top with remaining ¼ cup cilantro and serve.

*Substitution: I found that 2 teaspoons of Malaysian shrimp paste (found at Phil-Am) can be subbed for the 1 tablespoon of dried shrimp. Also, if you can't find either product, increase the fish sauce by 1 tablespoon as a replacement.

Tito Rad's Grill & Restaurant

The Filipino restaurant Tito Rad's operates as if a Filipino grandmother were at the helm in the kitchen (and she very well could be). A few blocks shy of what is considered Woodside's Little Manila territory, Tito Rad's constant turnover of tables in their no-frills environment is a strong testament to their food's popularity. Large groups of families descend on the restaurant to bask in the ethnic home-style menu. And that's the keystone of the cuisine. "Filipino cooking is all about home-style and home-cooking. When people come to the restaurant, we want them to feel like they're at home," says Nenette, sister of owner Mario Albenio. Lines out the door on weekends prompted Mario to purchase the larger space next door, which will be renovated and double the restaurant's size, and should be completed in the near future.

Chicken Adobo from Tito Rad's Grill and Restaurant. *(photo by Andrea Lynn)*

Any menu questions are happily fielded by the restaurant's waitstaff, which includes the very helpful and cheerful Nenette. "Filipino cooking is a combination of Spanish and Chinese; we use a lot of soy sauce and vinegar," explains Nenette. Case in point: the well-known Adobo, in which chicken or pork is braised in a vinegar-spiked soy sauce mixture. It's also been influenced by the plentiful seafood available in the Philippines. Grilled Tuna Jaw is massively popular among Filipino guests; Nenette advises to try the Grilled Tuna Belly instead, which has the same flavor without the bones. More must-tries are the Humba, pork braised in a sweet black bean sauce; the Sizzling Sisig, marinated pork belly with chiles; and the sour soups.

The sour soups are made tart by the addition of tamarind, and available in a variety of meats and Asian vegetables. Pancit Bam-I is sautéed egg noodles and rice noodles with the necessary veggies, pork, shrimp, and Chinese sausage. And it has to be sipped with their avocado shake; avocado is eaten like a fruit in the Philippines, according to Nenette. Don't miss out on a dessert of halo-halo—a mix of sweet beans, coconut, banana, and jackfruit tossed with shaved ice and plopped with ice cream scoops. Note that Nenette admits everything is cooked to order, just like you would at home, so don't expect speedy service (but I considered it a normal wait time, to be honest).

TITO RAD'S GRILL & RESTAURANT
Info: 49-20 Queens Blvd., Woodside; 718-205-7299; titorads.com

See You There: Take the 7 train to the 46th St. stop. Exit onto Queens Boulevard, walking toward 47th St. until you arrive at the restaurant. For an Authentic Experience: Try the Grilled Tuna Jaw or Grilled Tuna Belly, the tamarind-based sour soups, Humba, the Sizzling Sisig, and halo-halo for dessert.

Chicken Adobo (Adobong Manok) ■■■■■■■
Yield: 4 servings ■■■■■■■■■■■■■■■■

Any type of meat can be used in this famous Filipino dish, where it braises in a soy sauce and vinegar mixture. Taste your soy sauce first, dialing down the measurement to ⅓ cup in this recipe if it's extremely salty. Also, while not the norm, I enjoyed this with a side of couscous in place of rice. Recipe adapted from Mario Albenio.

> 1 (3-pound) chicken, cut into 8 pieces
> ½ cup soy sauce
> ¾ cup white vinegar
> 1 small white onion, sliced
> 6 cloves garlic, crushed
> 2 bay leaves
> ½ tablespoon whole black peppercorns
> 1 to 2 tablespoons canola oil
> 2 cups cooked rice, to serve

In a large heavy-duty pot, add chicken, soy sauce, vinegar, onion, garlic, bay leaves, and peppercorns. Bring to a boil over high heat. Cover, reduce heat to low, and simmer for 30 minutes. Using a slotted spoon, transfer chicken pieces from the pot. Bring the remaining liquid to a boil over high heat and cook until reduced by half, about 8 to 10 minutes. Meanwhile, coat the bottom of a large nonstick pan with oil and warm over high heat. Add chicken pieces and sauté until browned, about 3 minutes on each side. Serve hot with rice.

Oxtail Stew in Peanut Butter Sauce (Kare Kare) ■■
Yield: 4 servings ■■■■■■■■■■■■■■■■■

Most braised dishes come out of the pot with tender, succulent meat but overcooked, mushy vegetables. One of the beauties of this Oxtail Stew is that the veggies are cooked right at the end, delivering fresh crunchiness alongside soft oxtail. Oh, and peanut butter does indeed make everything better, oxtail stew included. Any extra peanut butter sauce is delicious mixed with Sriracha and shrimp paste and tossed with rice vermicelli noodles. Recipe adapted from Mario Albenio.

FOR THE OXTAIL STEW
4 pounds oxtail pieces
10 cups water
1 teaspoon kosher salt, plus more to taste
2 tablespoons canola oil
1 cup chopped onion
1 tablespoon finely minced garlic
1½ cups annatto water
½ cup rice flour
1 cup smooth peanut butter
1 small eggplant, peeled and sliced into bite-size pieces
½ pound green beans, cut into 2-inch lengths
½ pound baby bok choy, halved
freshly ground black petpper, to taste
Shrimp paste, to serve

FOR THE ANNATTO WATER
¼ cup plus 2 tablespoons annatto or achiote seeds
1½ cups water

Make the oxtail stew: In a large Dutch oven or heavy-duty large pot, add oxtail, water, and salt. Bring water to a boil over high heat, cover, and reduce the heat to medium-low. Let the oxtail cook in the simmering water until tender, about 2 to 3 hours. Transfer oxtail and broth to another container to reuse the Dutch oven.

Make the annatto water: Meanwhile, as the oxtails are nearing being tender, add the seeds and water to a bowl and crush them between your fingers to release the red color. Let stand for 30 minutes. Strain the water and discard the seeds.

In the empty Dutch oven, add oil and warm over medium-high heat. Add onion and sauté until soft, about 6 to 8 minutes. Stir in garlic and cook about 1 minute. Add annatto water and oxtail, and bring to a boil over high heat. Stir in the rice flour, peanut butter, and 4 cups of reserved oxtail broth, mixing well. Add in eggplant, green beans, and bok choy, making sure the vegetables are submerged in the sauce, so they will cook. Bring to a boil over high heat and simmer until veggies are tender, about 10 minutes. Season with salt and pepper to taste. Serve with a dab of shrimp paste.

Avocado Shake

Yield: 2 servings

The sugar in the avocado shake turns it into more of an end-of-the-meal craving, or maybe that's just my interpretation. At Tito Rad's, it was most certainly being consumed alongside dinner just like any other drink. I prefer this as a breakfast smoothie of sorts. Recipe inspired by Tito Rad's.

    1 ripe Hass avocado, peeled and sliced
    ¾ cup whole milk
    1 tablespoon sugar
    4 to 5 ice cubes
    1 teaspoon fresh lemon juice

Add all the ingredients into a blender. Purée until the ice is crushed and blended with the rest of the ingredients. Pour mixture into 2 glasses and serve.

FOOD SHOP: Ottomanelli & Son's Prime Meat Shop

What's better than a knowledgeable, old-school family butcher with fabulous cuts of meat? The same butcher who also weaves humorous stories into his daily routine (like of an encounter years ago with Michelle Pfeiffer). Meet Mike Ottomanelli, who helms the meat shop while his brother tends to the business at their new burger joint a block away. Mike says that, the most popular order is for the $9.99 porterhouse steak, but admits this could be attributed to the prominent sign hanging in the window. There's also the exotic selection, such as antelope patties, rattlesnake, and wild boar, with popularity rising lately in sales of venison, kangaroo, and alligator. If you haven't already ordered a marinated cut of meat, Mike will ask if you want their special spice blend sprinkled on your meat order. You do. He'll also field questions about the best way to cook your purchase, proving his theory about butchers: "Most supermarkets are trying to put us out of business," he says. "But they're not the same thing. You can't put a small store into a big store."

OTTOMANELLI & SON'S
Info: 6105 Woodside Ave., Woodside; 718-651-5544
See You There: Take the 7 train to the 61st St./Woodside stop.

S. Ottomanelli & Son's PRIME MEAT SHOP

(photo by Andrea Lynn)

Homemade spice blends at Ottomanelli & Son's. *(photo by Andrea Lynn)*

Three-Alarm Buffalo Chili

Yield: 6 servings

It doesn't get more American than chili, which Ottomanelli's gives a recipe for when asked how to use their buffalo stew meat. If you're not near a butcher, just substitute with beef stew meat. A note about chile powder: Penzey's Spices (penzeys.com) is a fabulous source for a range of good-quality chile powders. Also, make sure to know the difference between chile powder, which is a concentration of a specific type of powder like New Mexico chiles, and chili powder, which is a blend of spices, salt, and various types of chile powder. Make sure to taste the powder first before dumping it into the chili; you don't want to ruin your chili if it's spicier than you thought it was.

2 poblano chiles
2 tablespoons canola oil
3 pounds buffalo stew meat or beef chuck/stew meat,
    cut into 1-inch cubes
1 large onion, chopped
2 jalapeño peppers, finely chopped
4 cloves garlic, minced
2 large, ripe tomatoes, cored, seeded, and chopped
1 (28-ounce) can crushed tomatoes
1 (12-ounce) bottle beer
2 teaspoons dried oregano leaves
1 teaspoon freshly ground black pepper
1 teaspoon kosher salt
1½ tablespoons ground cumin
1 tablespoon ground sweet paprika
⅓ cup ground pasilla chile powder or ground
    New Mexico chile powder

To prepare the poblano chiles: Remove the stem from each chile. Using tongs, position chiles on a gas flame or almost touching an electric burner on high, and turn until each pepper is charred on all sides, about 10 to 15 minutes. Add chiles to a small bowl and cover with plastic wrap. Let stand for 15 to 20 minutes. When chiles are cool enough to handle, remove blistered skin from chiles. Cut chiles in half lengthwise and scrape out seeds and veins; finely chop them. (Keep the stems and veins if you prefer spicier food.)

To prepare the chili: Meanwhile, add 1 tablespoon oil to a heavy-duty 6- or 8-quart pot and warm over medium-high heat. Add only enough buffalo/beef cubes to fit the bottom of the pot, and cook until browned on each side, a few minutes per side. Transfer meat to a bowl and continue to brown remaining meat. Once all the meat has been browned and transferred to a bowl, reduce heat to medium. Add remaining 1 tablespoon oil, onion, and chopped jalapeños and stir often until onion is softened, about 6 to 8 minutes. Stir in garlic and cook about 1 minute. Stir in tomatoes, crushed tomatoes, chopped poblano, beer, and spices. Stir well, adding reserved meat back into the pot.

Bring to a boil, cover, reduce heat and simmer until meat is very tender when pierced, about 3 to 4 hours; stirring occasionally. Taste, and adjust seasonings, if necessary, before serving.

Fried fish for snacking at Phil-Am Food Mart. *(photo by Andrea Lynn)*

Food Shop: Phil-Am Food Mart

Wandering the aisles of Phil-Am, a few observations become apparent. Many Filipinos have a love affair with coconut and coconut-based products; there are more types of soy sauce than this soy sauce fiend knew was humanly possible; and snacks of fried fish piled high on plates abound.

Before even setting foot in the Filipino food shop, I had relied on Woodside resident/frequent Phil-Am Foods shopper Katrina Schultz Richter for advice on her favorite products: Barrio Fiesta brand shrimp paste and the lighter SilverSwan soy sauce (both used when she makes adobo). She also raved about Phil-Am's cooked foods, when available, like suman, the sweet sticky rice cooked and rolled in a palm leaf, which sells out early in the day, or turon, deep-fried spring-roll–wrapped bananas, which is only made every other Saturday (call in advance to see if it's the correct Saturday for serving). Employees are happy to field questions, like my inquiries on the Filipino pimento cheese (condensed milk and pineapple juice take this blend to a more tropical level) and the warning that Filipino soy sauces are a notch saltier than the Japanese variety.

Other finds include the mixed fruit makings for the halo-halo shaved ice dessert, a selection of longaniza sausages, salted duck eggs, and a row at the front of the store piled high with baked goodies such as sweet bread rolls that are just asking to be stuffed with the pimento cheese or longaniza (or both!).

PHIL-AM FOOD MART
Info: 70-02 Roosevelt Ave.; 718-899-1797
See You There: Take the 7 train to the 69th St. stop.

Filipino Pimento Cheese

Yield: 4 servings

Imagine this Southern gal's delight in seeing Phil-Am's refrigerated section stocked with versions of Filipino pimento cheese. I grew up on the addictive trio of cheddar cheese, mayo, and pimentos worshiped by Southerners, but hadn't a clue about other versions. The pineapple juice and condensed milk add sweetness to the mixture. Smear pimento cheese on crackers or celery sticks, toss into scrambled eggs, top a burger or hot dog, or wedge between two pieces of cornbread. Recipe adapted from Phil-am Food Mart.

⅓ cup mayonnaise
¼ cup condensed milk
½ cup pimentos or roasted red peppers, finely chopped
2 tablespoons pineapple juice
¼ teaspoon freshly ground pepper
Kosher salt, as needed
2 cups freshly grated sharp cheddar cheese or
    queso de bola

In a medium bowl, add mayonnaise, condensed milk, pimentos, pineapple juice, pepper, and salt. Add cheddar cheese and, using a fork, mash to combine mixture into a chunky paste. Add more mayo, if needed. Taste, and add salt, if needed. (The pimento cheese can also be made in the food processor, as they do at Phil-Am for more of a cohesive consistency: Cut the cheese into small chunks and whirl all the ingredients together until a paste forms.)

QUEENS FOOD PRO: Katrina Schultz Richter, founder of Queens County Market

What made you move to Queens and how long have you lived here? I grew up in Queens; first in Corona during my grade-school years and next in Flushing for middle school and high school. In my adulthood, I've lived in Sunnyside, Woodside, and Rego Park.

Name the reasons you love Queens: 1) Quality of life: Living in an affordable and spacious apartment that actually qualifies as a true one or two bedroom. 2) Roosevelt Avenue: The avenue of dreams. Also, the avenue of tacos, tortas, fried chicken (Korean, Filipino, Central American), momos, and empanadas! 3) Home: It's my hometown so there's always a lot of love in that.

Queens County Market founder, Katrina Schultz Richter. *(photo by Alexander Richter)*

What's your Queens claim to food fame? My start in the food industry was here in Queens so it was natural for me to launch a business in the same borough that I grew up in. After working in the industry for over a decade, I recognized the endless challenges that entrepreneurs face when starting their business and navigating the complicated and competitive food industry in New York City. Queens County Market (queenscountymarket.com) was launched to provide business support to first-time entrepreneurs. Our market provides an affordable retailing outlet for local producers to launch their food business and increase distribution to the diverse and vibrant neighborhoods in Queens.

Any favorite Queens memories? I don't think it's one particular memory in Queens, but growing up here, I was exposed to many cultures, all at a young age. It was at friends' birthday parties that I tried Indian curry, Greek leg of lamb, or Dominican empanadas for the first time. I also remember my fifth-grade teacher passing out matzo and potato latkes to the class, giving us a taste of traditional Jewish foods. I think it was this diversity in school that shaped me to become an open and adventurous eater.

Describe your ideal eating day in Queens: A gratuitous day of eating in Queens starts with a traditional Filipino breakfast at Krystal's in Woodside, mofongo for lunch at La Cabana in Corona, an afternoon chai from Kabir's in Jackson Heights, Chao Thai for dinner, and for dessert, a stop at Lemon Ice King of Corona.

What is a traditional Filipino breakfast exactly? I define a traditional Filipino breakfast as one with rice! Typically, a protein such as longaniza (sausage), danggit (a type of fish typically fried crispy) or tocino (cured bacon) + sinangag (garlic fried rice) + itlog (fried egg). This can be abbreviated to LongSiLog or DaSiLog or ToSiLog depending on what you order.

What type of non-food activities do you like to do in Queens or do you recommend others do? I love recommending a Mets game to visitors! Also, take a stroll at Socrates Sculpture Park or Astoria Park. Explore the abandoned battery at Fort Totten. Sunbathe in Rockaway Beach or take in the city views at Gantry Plaza State Park in Long Island City. Just make sure to include a subway ride on the 7 train to Flushing and eat on Main Street.

Name something you've only been able to find in a specific Queens location: Filipino grocery items like datu puti vinegar, fish sauce, and shrimp paste from Phil-Am Foods in Woodside.

What are a few under-the-radar food places in Queens? There's a Jamaican spot that makes a fantastic plate of spicy, super-tender Jamaican jerk chicken. It's near LaGuardia airport and that's all I'm saying!

Let's say you had to move out of the country: What would be your last meal in Queens? There would be too many! Peruvian chicken (with green sauce!) from Pio Pio, potato knish from Knish Nosh, a gyro from BZ Grill, pork soup dumplings and Shanghai noodles from Joe's Shanghai. I can go on. . . .

Any specific dishes from Queens restaurants that you've always wanted to make at home? Those pancakes from LIC Market! They've got the perfect balance of crispy outside and fluffy goodness inside. I'm all for carbs so there are definitely days of waking up and needing those pancakes, stat! (Author note: LIC Market's lips are sealed as to what makes their pancakes so magical. Which just means you'll have to add them to your list of Queens restaurants to try.)

Elmhurst street offerings. *(photo by Andrea Lynn)*

ELMHURST

Pad Kra Prao with Crispy Pork at Chao Thai.
(photo by Andrea Lynn)

ELMHURST

Within the span of a few days, I kept hearing about Chao Thai. First, from Scott Wong and Julie Wong of JoJu Modern Vietnamese Sandwiches, and then later from Daniel Yi at Salt & Fat. Daniel backpacked through Southeast Asia for a spell, and equates **Chao Thai** (and their sister location, **Chao Thai Too**, just one block away) with how food tasted in Thailand. He recommends their papaya salad and green curry. A cozy restaurant with fiery, authentic dishes, Chao Thai is a slice of Elmhurst's reigning ethnic food authenticity. You see, Elmhurst is home to a growing contingent of Thai immigrants, and Chao Thai is far from the only Thai standout in the neighborhood. **Ayada** transports diners to Bangkok with its authentic cuisine. "I knew Ayada was a serious Thai restaurant when I started weeping at my table," wrote the *New York Times'* Ligaya Mishan. "It was thrilling: So much of the Thai food in New York is docile, its spice neutered in a bid for Western palates. There were no such concessions here." Wander throughout the Asian food markets like **Thai Grocery**, along with **U.S. Supermarket** and **Hong Kong Supermarket,** making it easy to score Asian condiments in this neighborhood. Other Southeast Asian pockets make an appearance, like Indonesia, reflected in restaurants like **Pondok Jakarta** and **Upi Jaya** in a stretch of blocks referred to as "Little Indonesia," plus Vietnamese treasures **Pho Bang Restaurant** and **JoJu Modern Vietnamese Sandwiches**.

Lemongrass Chicken Banh Mi Sandwich
at JoJu Modern Vietnamese Sandwiches.
(photo by Andrea Lynn)

JoJu Modern Vietnamese Sandwiches

When the banh mi sandwich rage hit a handful of years ago, I wasn't the only Queens resident desperate for a location in the borough. Julie Wong and her brother-in-law, Scott Wong, were exasperated by trekking from Queens to Manhattan to get their banh mi fix. That's when they merged their restaurant industry talents to give Queens a taste of the Vietnamese sandwich. "I think Manhattan is more seen as a hangout place. Queens is more like, 'Oh, that's where you live,'" Julie says of her hometown. The duo was the first to bring the sandwich into Queens, and they've been going strong for three years now.

The banh mi is more than just a sandwich; it's a blend of cultures, according to Scott. It's the history of Western and Eastern cuisine merging through food: a Vietnam-French fusion, as a French baguette is piled high with Vietnamese components, liked pickled vegetables and Vietnamese ham. "Oh, and it tastes good," Scott adds. JoJu's sandwich combinations are split down the middle between traditional, like lemongrass chicken, classic pâté, BBQ pork, grilled pork chop, and the duo's modern spins and experimentations such as pork belly and the Korean-influenced beef bulgogi (which also nabs the most popular award).

Sandwich essentials include the pickled shredded carrots and daikon on a French baguette or the softer Italian bread, plus cilantro leaves, jalapeno slices, and thin cucumber wedges. And don't forget a slather of mayonnaise, which gives needed moisture to the sandwich. In Vietnam, there aren't any big manufacturers of mayonnaise, so the Wongs say most Vietnamese people make a homemade batch. While the shop is buzzing particularly at dinnertime, in Vietnam, banh mis are typically sold in a smaller size as a lunch or snack.

When plotting potential sides for the sandwiches, the Wongs devised a melding of Asian and American cuisines: banh mi fries and kimchee fries. The banh mi is bathed in an addictive green sauce that Julie says was inspired by Peruvian green sauces, like Pio Pio's on page 163. Just like the sandwiches, the fries can be ordered "loaded" (topped with the runny yolk of a fried egg). The new menu items have started a friendly battle over which one is the best, with my vote going to the banh mi (it's that green sauce that puts it over the edge, in my opinion). Also, devour a Vietnamese Iced Coffee with your meal, made with New Orleans' chicory-coffee blend from Café du Monde, the best mimic of the bitter-strong coffee made in Vietnam.

JOJU MODERN VIETNAMESE SANDWICHES
Info: 83-25 Broadway, Elmhurst; 347-808-0887; jojuny.com

See You There: Take the R/M train to Elmhurst Avenue, exiting at the Broadway-Elmhurst Avenue intersection. Travel along Broadway toward Whitney Ave. to reach the restaurant.

For an Authentic Experience: Order the Classic Banh Mi (with Vietnamese ham, headcheese, and pâté), Lemongrass Chicken Banh Mi, BBQ Pork, or Grilled Pork Chop. Make sure to get a Vietnamese Iced Coffee, bubble tea, or one of the quirkier drink selections like the Iced Pickled Lemon Soda.

Lemongrass Chicken Banh Mi ■■■■■■■■■

Yield: 4 sandwiches ■■■■■■■■■■■■■■■

There's a bit of advance work in making this sandwich. The pickled vegetables need a couple of days to soak in the vinegar mixture, and the chicken needs to marinate in lemongrass. My way to combat this is to shorten the time by preparing both 24 hours beforehand. As far as purchasing the lemongrass, the Wongs prefer the more reliably available frozen lemongrass. As someone who can never find lemongrass when a recipe calls for it, I thought a block of frozen lemongrass was ingenious (and nabbed it at the nearby U.S. Supermarket). The Wongs—and I—are all part of the dark meat fan club when it comes to chicken with a juicier experience. Recipe adapted from Julie Wong and Scott Wong.

FOR THE PICKLED VEGETABLES
1½ cup sugar
2¼ cups white vinegar
3½ cups water
2 cups grated daikon
2 cups grated carrots

FOR THE CHICKEN
⅓ cup soy sauce
2 tablespoons fish sauce
1½ tablespoons honey
2 tablespoons chopped lemongrass
1½ pounds boneless, skinless chicken thighs

TO ASSEMBLE
4 small, sandwich-size French baguettes or Italian bread
    (or about 8-inch sections cut from full-size versions)
Mayonnaise, as needed
2 English cucumbers, peeled and thinly sliced
2 jalapeños, thinly sliced
1 bunch cilantro, washed, dried, and stems discarded

Prepare the pickled vegetables: To make the pickled vegetables, add sugar, vinegar, and water in a medium pot. Bring to a boil over high heat, and stir until sugar is dissolved. Remove from heat, and stir in grated daikon and carrots. Transfer to a container and refrigerate for a minimum of 24 hours, with 2 to 3 days being ideal, according to the Wongs.

Prepare the chicken: In a ziplock bag, add soy sauce, fish sauce, honey, and lemongrass. Use a spoon to combine mixture together. Add chicken, seal the plastic bag, and refrigerate for about 24 hours.

To serve, preheat a large nonstick sauté pan over medium-high heat. Add the chicken, making sure not to overcrowd the pan (cooking in batches, if necessary). Cook the chicken, flipping with tongs, until fully cooked, about 5 minutes per side. Remove from pan, let cool slightly, and slice on the bias. To assemble the sandwiches, slice the bread lengthwise. Spread desired amount of mayonnaise on both sides. Layer sandwich with chicken slices, cucumbers, jalapeños, pickled vegetables, and cilantro leaves. Cut in half and serve.

Ayada Thai

Shrimp with Thai Chile Sauce ■■■■■■■■■■
Yield: 4 to 6 appetizers ■■■■■■■■■■■■■■■

Time Out New York declared Ayada Thai's raw shrimp salad as one of one hundred must-have tastes in New York City. Raw, cleaned shrimp are topped with a Thai chile, lime and fish sauce purée, and a thin slice of garlic. Bitter melon and carrot shreds serve both as garnish and also a way to tame your mouth from the escalading heat. The salad is based on the Thai dish Gung Che Num Pa. While I have no qualms about eating raw shrimp at the restaurant, I was a little hesitant to do so on my own, especially considering that fishmongers I asked were skeptical about raw shrimp consumption. I used cooked shrimp in this recipe inspired by Ayada Thai's dish. If you want the full sashimi experience, purchase sashimi-grade tuna, slice into thin pieces, and drizzle with a bit of the sauce.

> 1½ pounds medium or large shrimp, peeled and deveined
> 1 scallion, roughly chopped
> 10 to 15 Thai chiles (depending on desired spice level), stemmed
> 4 cloves garlic
> 2 tablespoons fresh lime juice
> 2 tablespoons fish sauce
> 1 tablespoon extra-virgin olive oil

Bring a medium pot of water to a boil over high heat. Add shrimp to the boiling water and cook just until pink—about 2 to 3 minutes, depending on size. Remove shrimp, and drain in a colander.

In the bowl of a food processor, add scallion, chiles, garlic, lime juice, and fish sauce. Purée until combined, about 30 seconds, pouring olive oil down the feeder tube. Taste, adjusting any ingredients if needed. Pour Thai chile sauce into a small bowl and serve with shrimp for dipping (just a small dab is needed since the sauce is ultra-spicy).

AYADA THAI
Info: 77-08 Woodside Ave. in Elmhurst; 718-424-0844; ayadathaiwoodside.com.

See You There: From Manhattan, take the R/E or the F/M subway into Queens, getting off at the Roosevelt Avenue–Jackson Avenue exit. Walk south on 74th St. and then make a left onto Woodside Ave. to reach the restaurant.

FOOD SHOP: U.S. Supermarket

There are two main entrances to this sprawling Asian grocery store, which makes entering and exiting slightly confusing. But it's a small price to pay for the expansive selection of Asian goods. The vast seafood and fish selection (and prices) are a revelation: bins of live crabs, frogs, lobsters, and more that can be killed and filleted or steamed on the spot, if desired.

Fresh vegetables include the more unusual, like durian, raw peanuts, green papaya, champagne mangos, and more. There's also recipe essentials for Asian cooking, such as shrimp paste, frozen minced lemongrass, palm sugar, and tamarind paste.

I asked Julie Wong and Scott Wong, owners of JoJu Modern Vietnamese Sandwiches, for tips on what they purchase from the Asian U.S. Supermarket. Julie stocks up on a variety of snacks, including little jars of fried anchovies. They both raved about the selection of fresh vegetables, exotic sauces straight from Asia, and other essentials like the enormous selection of rice paper ("It's the most I've ever seen in an aisle in the city," says Julie.) Take their advice and just walk up and down each aisle to explore. There's also equipment like rice cookers and the Vietnamese coffee drip filter used to make Vietnamese coffee, along with the essential Café du Monde coffee.

U.S. SUPERMARKET
Info: 82-66 Broadway

See You There: Take the M or R train to the Elmhurst Ave. exit.

La Esquina del Camaron Mexicano

Underneath a weathered, peeling awning for Roosevelt Grocery Corp. in Elmhurst, a line snakes around the corner patiently waiting for Pedro Rodriguez to set up his stand. They've been craving Pedro's seafood cocktail all week; what's another fifteen minutes?

On weekends, the southeast corner of Roosevelt Avenue and 80th Street morphs into a seafood paradise, as Pedro's Mexican-style seafood cocktails put the American version to shame. Whole pink shrimp and bites of tender octopus are packed into a choice of small, medium, or large containers, priced $6 to $12. When available, plump oysters can be added into the mix for an extra charge, and they're well worth the price. Pedro then pours his secret tomato-based concoction over the seafood, adding a splash of clam juice, lime juice, and olive oil. Avocado slices, white onions, and cilantro are spooned on top, with a dose of Valentina hot sauce (his favorite), if desired.

Pedro had thoughts about transitioning to a less physically taxing career than his current day job as a carpenter. "Since moving to this country, I learned to do all kinds of things I didn't do before, like painting and carpentry," he says of his two decades in the United States. But he yearned for the food of Mexico City, thinking that his future lay in seafood *cócteles*. "Every time I get the chance, I eat it. I love it," Pedro says. Two years ago, he took the plunge on his dream, earning a food certification and opening a weekend business from a cooler outside Elmhurst's Glober Market, which is where I first encountered him. It was a cold February weekend when I first sampled his seafood cocktail on the way to another stop; the refreshing delicacy of it all danced in my head for months after.

One year later, Pedro expanded to his current larger space, even adding an assistant to keep up with demand. He sets up between 11 and 11:30 a.m. and stays until his seafood is sold out, which is sometimes in a matter of a few hours. His menu is an homage to the seafood cocktails he remembers from Mexico, and they've become so sought-after that he goes through eighty pounds of shrimp and octopus a day. His salivating customers are a mix of Mexican-Americans looking for a taste of their heritage, and newcomers unfamiliar with the Mexican seafood delicacy.

The Mexican seafood cocktail provides more than a livelihood for Pedro; it's an opportunity to show New Yorkers another side of Mexican food, which is often thought of as just tacos and tortas. As an incentive to both new and loyal customers, he plans to add calamari to the seafood mix in the near future, and start operating on weekdays inside the Roosevelt Grocery.

LA ESQUINA DEL CAMARON MEXICANO
Info: Southeast Corner of Roosevelt Ave. and 80th St. in Elmhurst; currently, it's just open on weekends.

See You There: Take the 7 train to the 82nd St. stop.

Mexican-Style Seafood Cocktail

Pedro's lips are sealed as far as to how he makes his special tomato-based sauce for the seafood cocktail, but here's a close adaptation. Recipe adapted from Pedro Rodriguez.

    1 teaspoon kosher salt
    1 pound medium shrimp, deveined and shelled
    1 (1½- to 2-pound) small octopus, cleaned, head removed,
        and cut into tentacles
    1 cup water
    4 cloves garlic
    1 bay leaf
    1 lemon
    2 cups tomato juice
    1 tablespoon tomato paste
    2 tablespoons clam juice
    2 teaspoons sugar
    Juice of 3 limes

2 (8-ounce) jars good-quality shucked oysters, drained
1 tablespoon extra-virgin olive oil
¼ cup finely diced white onion
¼ cup cilantro sprigs
1 avocado, diced
Valentina hot sauce, to serve (optional)
Saltine crackers, to serve

Bring a medium pot of water and ½ teaspoon salt to a boil over high heat. Add shrimp, cooking 2 to 3 minutes until completely pink. Drain in a colander. Let shrimp cool and then refrigerate in an airtight container a minimum of 4 hours.

In a medium pot, add ½ teaspoon salt, octopus tentacles, water, garlic, and bay leaf. Halve the lemon and squeeze lemon juice into pot, then add lemon halves. Bring to a boil over high heat; when boiling, cover with lid, and reduce heat to medium-low so mixture is simmering. Cook until octopus is tender, about 45 minutes to 1 hour. Let octopus cool in cooking liquid. When cool, remove from liquid and pat dry with paper towel. Cut the tentacles into 1-inch pieces, transfer to an airtight container, and refrigerate a minimum of 4 hours.

Mexican-Style Seafood Cocktail at La Esquinita del Camaron Mexicano.
(photo by Janis Turk)

When ready to serve, add tomato juice, tomato paste, clam juice, sugar, and lime juice into a medium bowl and whisk to combine.

In a large bowl, add reserved shrimp, octopus, and oysters. Add olive oil to seafood, and mix to combine. Divide seafood mixture between 4 bowls. Then, pour the tomato-based sauce into each bowl almost to the top of the seafood (all the liquid may not be used). Garnish each seafood cocktail with onion, cilantro, and avocado. Serve with hot sauce and saltine crackers.

Elmhurst Mex Grocery Company

Cactus, Orange, and Pineapple Juice ▪▪▪▪▪▪
Yield: 5 cups ▪▪▪▪▪▪▪▪▪▪▪▪▪▪▪▪▪▪

If you're craving any fruit or vegetable in liquid form Elmhurst Mex Grocery Juice Stand probably has will have it, from papaya-apple-pear juice to honeydew smoothies to tamarind aguas frescas. My favorite was a mix of cactus purée with pineapple and orange—so much so that I decided to re-create it after always seeing cactus leaves at my grocery store.

    4 to 5 medium nopales (cactus leaves)
    2½ cups chopped pineapple chunks
    2 cups fresh orange juice (about 5 medium oranges)
    4 to 5 ice cubes

Carefully hold the bottom of the cactus leaf paddle, and run your knife upward across the cactus leaf to scrap off the needles. Turn it over and remove needles from the other side. Cut the outer edges off the cactus, since those are nearly impossible to remove by scraping. Continue to clean remaining cactus and then chop into enough pieces to measure about 2 cups.

Add chopped cactus into a blender, along with pineapple, orange juice, and ice cubes. Blend until mixture is puréed, about 1 to 2 minutes. Pour into glasses and serve.

ELMHURST MEX GROCERY COMPANY
Info: 80-03 Broadway in Elmhurst; 718-424-0107

See You There: From Manhattan, take the R train into Queens, getting off at the Elmhurst Ave. subway stop. Walk northwest on Broadway until you reach Elmhurst Mex Grocery Company.

Elmhurst Walking Tour

Take the M or R train to Elmhurst Avenue. Walk northwest on Broadway 2½ blocks to Ⓐ **Elmhurst Mex Grocery Co.** (80-03 Broadway; 718-424-0107) for natural juices, like my fave, the Cactus, Pineapple, and Orange creation. It's an endless selection of almost anything you can think of, like Beet with Orange and Apple, Papaya with Apple and Pear, and smoothies galore from Coconut to Honeydew. Cross to the other side of Broadway, make a soft left onto Woodside Avenue and walk 3 to 4 blocks to Ⓑ **Upi Jaya** (76-04 Woodside Avenue; 718-458-1807) where the highlights of this family run Indonesian restaurant include the fiery Rendang Padang, where the beef braises for at least 7 hours, or Ikan Pepes, a whole red snapper cooked with chiles and herbs while packed tightly in a banana leaf. Then wander through the neighboring Ⓒ **Thai Grocery** (76-13 Woodside Ave.; 917-769-6168) for any Thai product needs like tamarind paste, chiles, shrimp paste, and more. Walk back to Broadway and make a right. Head to the Vietnamese Ⓓ **Pho Bang** (82-90 Broadway; 718-205-1500) to slurp your way through soups like Tai Nam Gau Gan Sach (beef soup with rice noodles). If there's a standing-room-only crowd at Pho Bang, go across the street to Ⓔ **Uncle Zhou** (83-29 Broadway; 718-393-0888) for Henan Province-based Chinese standouts like Spicy Beef Knife-Shaved Noodle Soup. Continue on Broadway two blocks to Ⓕ **Starry Bakery & Café** (83-09 Broadway; 718-806-1528) for a shaved ice (or what they call a snow ice). While the shaved iced in Flushing has more elements, this snow ice is the perfect sweet cool-down at the end of a hot summer day.

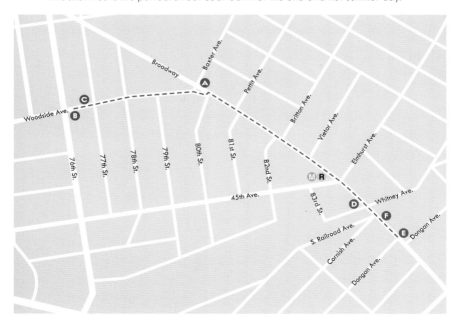

Mole de olla (beef and chile broth) at Tacos al Suadero, one of the many Mexican and Latin American food establishments in Elmhurst. *(photo by Andrea Lynn)*

QUEENS FOOD PRO: Lesley Tellez, Elmhurst-based cookbook author and owner of Eat Mexico Culinary Tours

Name the reasons you love Queens: 1) The food! 2) Hearing different languages on the street every day. 3) Access to trains that take me where I need to go. 4) Affordability of housing, compared to Manhattan and Brooklyn.

What do you think is the biggest misconception about Queens? People think it's too far to visit. Then they come on the train and say, "You know, it didn't take that long to get here."

What's the most surprising experience (foodwise) you've had in Queens? The first time I went to Biang! in Flushing and had a bowl of their cold noodle salad. It tingled in my mouth—I hadn't had Sichuan peppers before.

Any favorite Queens memories? Visiting Terraza 7 and dancing salsa into the wee morning hours with a gay Ecuadorian couple and a waiter from Mexico City.

Describe your ideal eating day in Queens: At this moment? Breakfast: congee with youtiao and a side of roast pork at Shun Wong, which is very close to my house. Lunch: Big chunks of fried eggplant, with chicken and basil at Chao Thai Too. Snack: Grilled Meat Skewer from the food cart at Whitney and Broadway, followed by bubble tea from Quickly. Dinner: Beer and snacks at Sweet Afton in Astoria.

What type of non-food activities do you like to do in Queens or do you recommend others to do? Riding my bike around the neighborhood, when the weather's good. It's fun to ride to Sunnyside or Woodside and stop for a pint somewhere; spending sunny summer days at Rockaway Beach; getting in some good yoga at The Yoga Room.

Fall foliage in Queens.
(photo by Andrea Lynn)

Wok stir-frying at Phayul.
(photo by Janis Turk)

JACKSON HEIGHTS

For decades, Jackson Heights has been known as a mecca of Indian restaurants, from the well-known Indian buffet at **Jackson Diner** to the snacky chaats and neon-orange sugary sweets at **Rajbhog Sweets and Snacks**. But this Indian population has dwindled in recent years, moving to other parts of New York and taking their restaurants with them. Instead, a new culinary ethnic concentration is in Jackson Heights: the lesser-known Himalayan cuisine, which includes Nepalese and Tibetan versions. Jeff Orlick, Jackson Heights food guide and overall neighborhood expert, equates this with the classic immigrant experience of New York. "I see a lot of the same things happening in Queens that remind me of the immigrant experiences fifty and one hundred years ago. In Little India, the actual Indians have mostly moved out to the suburbs and become Americans," he says. "This is the same thing that happened with Jewish food from early in the last century. When the large populations of Jews were arriving, they were only familiar with their own types of food—that's what they were comfortable with, and those were the types of businesses that thrived. Just like what I am seeing in Jackson Heights, the Himalayan businesses have tremendous popularity—they are very recent immigrants and this is the type of trade that they are comfortable with." This new wave of food in Jackson Heights includes several popular restaurants under the Himalayan umbrella: **Himalayan Yak**, **Little Tibet**, **Tibet Mobile**, **Phayul**, and more. Like other parts in Queens, a sizeable Latino population has also flexed its muscle through clusters of Ecuadorian food carts, tamale sellers, and more. Maria Piedad Cano helms a well-known, evening-only cart on Roosevelt Avenue and is known by her fans as **The Arepa Lady**, causing *New York* magazine to rave that "Maria Piedad Cano might be New York's most revered street vendor."

Himalayan Yak

For those (like myself) whose knowledge of Himalaya is limited to the fact that Mt. Everest is lodged within the Himalayan mountains, its cuisine is almost like a history lesson, thanks to Himalayan Yak manager Gyaltsen Gurung.

First, understand that five countries lay claim to different parts of the mountain range: Bhutan, India, and Nepal claim the majority, with China and Pakistan having small slivers of the land. This knowledge makes tackling a menu like Himalayan Yak's easier, as it is divided into Nepali, Tibetan, and Indian selections.

Think of Nepal as more of a hodgepodge of different ethnicities. Gurung equates it to Queens: "a lot of people from different places, like you see in Queens." Samayabajee is a traditional Nepali platter with various pickles (radish pickles, potato pickles), soybeans, and meat—reflecting the Nepali people's taste for spiciness and pickled items, similar to Indian dishes. The cuisine is also known for its beaten rice, which is a flattened, crispier counterpart to white rice.

According to Gurung, Tibetan standbys are the dumplings, called momos, and because of the Himalayas' limited vegetation, the most you'll get in the form of a salad is a garnish of cucumbers and carrots on the side. The cuisine is more focused on meat, like the blood sausage gyuma. "We made little changes to the recipe, but it tastes pretty much the same [as in Tibet]," he says. Another specialty is the wobbly Laphing, or mung jelly.

True to the culture, internal organs of animals are a hefty part of the restaurant's appetizers. "We use more internal organs so that we don't waste any parts," he says. Other parts of the animal can be preserved, but internal organs must be consumed right way. "We don't have refrigeration systems like that back home, and I mean Tibet especially."

Napalese dumplings, are practically identical to the Tibetan ones, with the latter being larger and heartier in its filled meat. Choose meat or veggies—anything can go inside a momo, as long as it is mixed with the required onion, garlic, and spices. Yak, which has beef-tasting similarities, is a must for the cuisine. The restaurant's yak comes farm-raised in the U.S. but Gurung admits it doesn't stand up to the grass-fed, wild-roaming yak in his homeland. When Himalayans migrate to other countries, most discover that Indian food mimics the food style of home the closest. So they soon begin to add Indian dishes into their repertoire, hence the inclusion on menus like Himalayan Yak's. But for a purely more cultural food experience, go for the Himalayan and Tibetan selections.

HIMALAYAN YAK
Info: 72-20 Roosevelt Ave., Jackson Heights; 718-779-1119; himalayanyak.com

See You There: Take the M or R train into Queens to the Roosevelt Ave./Jackson Heights stop. Exit at the Broadway and 73rd St. exit, traveling south on 73rd St. until reaching the restaurant, just a couple minutes.

For an Authentic Experience: Try the Samayabajee platter as an appetizer, along with Laphing (mung bean jelly) and Gyuma (Tibetan-style sausage). Then go for the Momos; Shapta with Yak; and manager Gyaltsen Gurung's favorite, Himalayan Yak: sliced beef tongue, called Cheley. Note that everything is eaten at the same time, versus the soup-salad-entrée order popular in the United States.

The ornate front of Himalayan Yak. *(photo by Andrea Lynn)*

Shapta (Sautéed Sliced Beef)

Yield: 4 servings

While this dish is traditionally served with Tibetan bread called bhaley, rice is an adequate replacement. Or, serve it with the Sho-Go Khatsa (page 160), like I do, despite Gurung trying to explain to me that they're both entrées and not meant to be eaten together (I am assuming based on the spice level alone). Excess beef broth can be used for Beef Soup with Potatoes (page 169). A tip for getting the beef sliced as thinly as possible: Place the steak into the freezer for 20 to 30 minutes. The steak will firm up, making it easier to slice. Recipe adapted from Himalayan Yak.

3 to 4 cups beef stock
6 cloves garlic, crushed
1½ pounds top sirloin steak, thinly sliced
1 tablespoon freshly grated ginger
1½ tablespoons canola oil
1 large red onion, chopped
1 green bell pepper, seeded and sliced
1 red bell pepper, seeded and sliced
2 teaspoons chili powder
2 teaspoons ground turmeric
½ teaspoon red hot chile flakes
½ teaspoon kosher salt
1 or 2 jalapeños, thinly sliced (optional)
2 cups cooked rice, to serve

Using a wok or a large deep skillet, add beef stock, crushed garlic cloves, and thinly sliced sirloin. Bring to a boil over high heat, cover with a lid, reduce heat to medium and let the meat cook until tender, about 20 to 30 minutes. (Cooking time can vary depending on the thickness of the beef.) Use a slotted spoon to remove the garlic and beef. Reserve broth. Let garlic cool, and then mince to make a paste with ginger.

Wipe out the wok or skillet to reuse, making sure it is dry. Warm oil over medium-high heat, and add onion and bell peppers. Cook, stirring, until softened, about 5 to 8 minutes. Add in reserved beef and garlic, ginger paste, spices, jalapeños, and ½ cup reserved broth. Stir to combine and cook until broth and spices have reduced to coat the beef. Taste, adjusting seasonings if needed. Serve with rice or another side.

Sho-Go Khatsa (Aloo Dum) ■ ■ ■ ■ ■ ■ ■ ■ ■ ■

When trying to get tips from Himalayan Yak manager Gyaltsen Gu-rung on this potato recipe, he kind of shrugged and said, "It's just cooked potatoes." But it's so much more than that, having moved up my recipe queue to become a favorite side dish. So much flavor is pumped into this that serving it with a tamer, albeit more boring main dish like sautéed chicken breasts brings a bit of uniqueness to dinner. Gurung also introduced me to Panch Phoran, a spice blend of seeds like cumin, nigella, black mustard, and fennel. Available at Jackson Heights' Patel Brothers or online, it's now my number one potato seasoner. Recipe adapted from Himalayan Yak.

    2 pounds baby red potatoes
    8 garlic cloves
    8 to 10 dried chile de árbol peppers
       (or another type of spicy whole chile pepper)
    1 tablespoon canola oil
    ½ teaspoon kosher salt
    ½ teaspoon ground turmeric
    1 teaspoon Panch Phoran
       (or 1 teaspoon cumin seeds or fennel seeds)
    1 teaspoon black sesame seeds, for garnish

Add the potatoes to a large pot and cover with water. Bring to a boil over high heat and then add garlic cloves and chile peppers. Let cook until potatoes are just barely tender, when a knife poked into the potato is still just hitting resistance, around 12 to 15 minutes. At the 10-minute mark, use a slotted spoon to remove garlic and chile peppers from the water, and place into a bowl. Transfer potatoes to a colander, saving about ⅓ cup the potato water. Cool down the potatoes by running cold water over them for a few minutes.

While you're letting the potatoes cool down so they can be handled, add the reserved chiles and garlic into the bowl of a food processor or blender. Purée until smooth, adding the reserved water down the feeder tube, just until chile sauce is a desired consistency.

When the potatoes have cooled, use your hands to remove the peels. Cut the potatoes into small pieces. In a large sauté pan or a wok, warm the oil over high heat. Carefully add the potatoes, and stir-fry until potatoes are soft, about 5 minutes. When the potatoes are fully tender, stir in the reserved chile sauce, salt, turmeric and Panch Phoran. Let the sauce boil until it has reduced down to a sauce that coats the potatoes, just a few minutes. Garnish with sesame seeds and serve.

Pio Pio

While a little less authentic than other restaurants in this book, Pio Pio will always hold a special allure for me. The first time I tasted their chicken and green sauce at their original but cramped Rego Park location, I was addicted. The chicken was juicy and tender in a finger-licking kind of way, but it was the spicy green sauce that I couldn't get enough of. And I'm not alone in my quest to make this. Katrina Schultz Richter, founder of Queens County Market, described a fellow obsession with Peruvian green sauces, and Julie Wong, co-owner of JoJu Modern Vietnamese Sandwiches, harnessed her love for the sauce into a similar one that drenches a couple menu items, including the banh mi fries.

The restaurant now has a smattering of outlets around New York City, including this sprawling restaurant off Northern Boulevard. And Pio Pio does Peruvian food well, despite the added locations over the years. Start with sangria or a pisco cocktail and ceviche, and then go for the Matador combo of the rotisserie chicken with a few sides, including salchipapa, French fries mixed with hot dog slices (just trust me on the deliciousness of this). Be prepared to ask for a vat of the green sauce to take home and dabble on everything in sight. But then, you're in luck, because I have a similar recipe to meet all your Pio Pio needs.

PIO PIO
Info: 84-02 Northern Blvd., Jackson Heights; 718-426-4900

See You There: Take the 7 train into Flushing to the 82nd St./ Jackson Heights stop. Travel north on 82nd St. for about 10 minutes until hitting Northern Blvd.

Peruvian roasted chicken with Aji Verde at Pio Pio. *(photo by Janis Turk)*

Peruvian Roasted Chicken with Aji Verde (Green Sauce)

Yield: 4 servings

When I was working at *Chile Pepper* magazine, another editor and I decided to get to the bottom of the mystery sauce. At several Pio Pio restaurants, I would ask for the ingredients in different ways, either by asking outright ingredient questions or by feigning food allergies (I'm not proud of what this green sauce has made me do). The answers were across the board. As I wrote for *Serious Eats* when documenting my obsession, I had to face the reality that either *no one knew what was in the sauce*, the ingredients were top secret, or both. Every Peruvian restaurant has its own secret recipe for this mysterious condiment. Others have clamored to make their own favorite versions of the sauce, some swearing by a head of lettuce, evaporated milk, or black mint. This is the closest I could get cross-engineering style. If you can't find the aji Amarillo paste, which is found in Latin grocery stores and even regular supermarkets in the international aisle, just increase the jalapeño amount to three. Recipe inspired by Pio Pio.

FOR THE CHICKEN MARINADE
½ cup light beer
4 cloves garlic, minced
2 tablespoons freshly squeezed lime juice
2 tablespoons canola oil
2 teaspoons kosher salt
2 teaspoons ground paprika
1 teaspoon cumin
¾ teaspoon dried oregano
½ teaspoon freshly ground pepper
1 (3 to 3½ pound) whole chicken

FOR THE SAUCE
2 fresh jalapeños, including seeds and ribs, roughly chopped
1 tablespoon aji Amarillo paste
1 cup roughly chopped cilantro
2 tablespoons grated cotija cheese or Parmesan cheese
1 medium clove garlic, minced
1 tablespoon vegetable oil
1 teaspoon white vinegar
½ teaspoon lime juice
⅓ cup mayonnaise
Kosher salt and freshly ground black pepper

Make the chicken: In a large ziplock bag, add all the marinade ingredients. Use a spoon to combine and then add chicken. Seal and refrigerate for 12 to 24 hours.

To cook the chicken, preheat the oven to 425°F. Remove chicken from marinade, pat dry with paper towels, and place in a roasting pan. Cook chicken to an internal temp of 165°F, which will hover around 45 to 55 minutes of cooking time.

While chicken is resting, make the sauce: Combine jalapeños, aji Amarillo, cilantro, cheese, garlic, oil, vinegar, and lime juice in a blender or food processor. Blend on high speed until smooth paste forms. Add mayonnaise, salt, and pepper and blend until combined. Serve chicken with green sauce. Unused sauce can be stored in a covered container for up to 1 week (as if it will last that long).

Kababish

Don't be deterred by the snugness of this Pakistani restaurant—which also dabbles in Indian and Bangladeshi fare—or the counters in place of table seating. You want to eat at the restaurants where the immigrants go for a taste of their homeland, and this is it.

The slight slick of oil on the dishes at the counter is good—in fact, in India, this signals that the prepared food is of high quality. When Andrew Zimmern profiled the space on **Bizarre Foods**, he (of course) went for the craziest concoction: tawa kata-kat, a mix of goat brains, kidneys and heart spiced with chiles and ginger. Kababs like chicken, beef, or lamb are also available, but the star of the show is the gola kabab, with a rich, almost patélike consistency. Watch the cook squeeze and shape the meat around the metal skewer, whirling a string around it to keep it in place as it cooks away in the open-fire grill. It's served with some toasty warm naan—a chewy Indian flatbread—that can be seen stretching and baking in the back of the kitchen; the bread tempers the fiery explosion of the gola kabab. (On the way to Kababish, take a trip to Patel Brothers for a bottle of sugary sweet mango nectar which cuts the heat.)

KABABISH
Info: 70-64 Broadway, Jackson Heights; 718-565-5131

See You There: From Manhattan, take the R/M or the F/E subway into Queens, getting off at the Roosevelt Avenue-Jackson Avenue exit. Walk west on Broadway toward 72nd St., until reaching the restaurant.

(photo by Janis Turk)

Little Tibet

Tibetans have a love affair with soup, for good reason. "Tibet is at such a higher altitude. It's called 'the roof of the world.' People wanted something to keep them warm, so there are a lot of soup dishes," explains Little Tibet co-owner Tenzin Choenyi. "Even other dishes that would normally not be with the soup, we try to make it into a soup. Or, dishes like dumplings—every time we send out a dumpling, it usually comes with a soup to complement [it]." Indeed, Tibetan dumplings—called momos—aren't complete without a side of soup. And there even needs to be a bit of meaty liquid inside the dumpling. "It's a good dumpling if you bite it and the juice squirts out of it, so you have to wash your clothes," she says.

Butter tea is also a body-warmer for Tibetans. "So, originally, I'm sure that butter tea is made of, I mean, of course it's made of yak milk and yak butter, but now unless you go to the Bronx Zoo or where they keep their yaks, we won't get that. So, it's just milk, butter, and cream," says Tenzin, who has childhood memories of her mom churning butter tea in what's called a dong mo.

Tenzin and her fiancé, Lobsang Choephel, opened the restaurant (first called Zomsa) to serve their local community of Tibetans, and to attract those interested in the food. They merged their talents: Tenzin's decade of front-of-the-house restaurant experience and Tenzin's restaurant cooking experience preparing Thai food in India. Choephel explains, through his fiancée's translations, that to the normal palate, the simplicity of Tibetan cuisine could translate into blandness. "If it's beef soup, you can just taste the beef bone soup. You don't add a lot of things to it," he says. The Himalayan or Nepalese twists on the same dishes involve adding their own more aggressive spices.

Since Tibet is occupied by China, Tenzin's admits many people don't know about the culture. "So the food did not get a chance to be explored by people of the world because Tibet was repressed," she says. This new crop of restaurants in areas like Jackson Heights are bringing what she considers the first wave of attention to the cuisine. "Tibetan food, because the culture was so repressed, it did not get a chance to evolve. So I think the food that is coming out now from the restaurants, it's just the Tibetan Food 101 phase," she says.

LITTLE TIBET
Info: 72-19 Roosevelt Ave., Jackson Heights; 718-505-8423

See You There: Take the M or the R train into Queens to the Roosevelt Ave./Jackson Heights stop. Exit at the Broadway and 73rd St. exit, traveling south on 73rd St. until reaching the restaurant, just a couple minutes.

For an Authentic Experience: The Tibetan sausage in Gyuma, Momos, and Phingsha (a beef soup with vermicelli, potatoes, and mushrooms), and the Thenthuk (hand-pulled noodles with radishes and boy choy in a vegetable or beef broth) are not to be missed.

Shabhaley-making at Little Tibet. *(photo by Andrea Lynn)*

Shabhaley (Tibetan-style Empanadas)

Yield: 20 to 30 empanadas (depending on size)

Tenzin Choenyi stressed that Tibetans have a culture of simplicity, which is reflected in their food. Such is the case in this Tibetan-style empanada. The dough is just flour and water, kneaded until ready (and in this recipe, untraditionally kneaded in a food processor). The dough is then filled with ground beef on the fattier side (and then enhanced with a few splashes of olive oil) to get that meaty juiciness inside the dough. When rolling out the empanada dough, try to cut out as many rounds as possible; the dough can be kneaded and rolled out a second time but isn't quite as easy to work with. Recipe adapted from Tenzin and Lobsang.

FOR THE DOUGH
4 cups all-purpose flour
1 teaspoon kosher salt
1½ to 2 cups warm water

FOR THE MEAT FILLING
1 small onion, quartered
2 scallions
½ bunch cilantro, washed
½ teaspoon kosher salt
¼ teaspoon freshly ground pepper
2 tablespoons olive oil
½ pound (80 percent) lean ground beef
Canola oil, as needed
Hot sauce, to serve (optional)

In the bowl of a food processor, add flour, salt and 1½ cups water. Process until it all comes together as a gob of dough, adding water through the feeder tube until a ball of dough forms. Remove dough from the food processor, transferring onto a flour-dusted cutting board. Knead the dough a couple more times. Split dough into 2 balls, cover with plastic wrap and let rest.

Wash out the bowl of the food processor. Add onion, scallions, and cilantro, pulsing the mixture to make into a very fine dice. Be careful: you don't want to overprocess, because the onion will turn into a watery mess. (It's better to pull out large pieces of onion from the mixture than to overprocess.) Add salt, pepper, and oil; gently pulsing just a couple times to combine the mixture. Transfer to a bowl and combine with the raw ground beef using a spatula or your hands.

On the flour-dusted cutting board, use a rolling pin to roll out the dough to a thinness of ¼ inch to ½ inch. Using a circular cutter or a drinking glass, cut out circles. Use your fingers to slightly stretch out the dough to make slightly larger. On half the dough circle, add a spoonful of meat mixture. Close the dough to make a half-moon shape and use a fork to crimp the edges of the dough to keep in the filling while cooking. (The restaurant makes a lovely crimped design on the dough of their empanadas, but the fork is a much easier way for a dumpling novice to go. It's essential that the empanada is fully closed or the meat juices drip out during the cooking process which makes a mess.) Roll out the other ball of dough, repeating to cut and fill them.

Using a large sauté pan or a wok, add enough canola oil for at least 1 inch of oil. Warm over medium-high heat, and cook empanadas until golden-brown on each side, around 2 to 3 minutes per side. According to Tenzin, heat the oil until it gets hot, but avoid letting it get super-hot. Test 1 or 2 empanadas by cutting them open to make sure the meat is cooked to determine cooking time. Then cook remaining empanadas.

Transfer the cooked empanadas to a paper towel-lined plate and continue cooking until all the dumplings have been cooked. Serve with hot sauce, if desired.

Phingsha (Beef Soup with Potatoes) ■■■■■■■

This traditional comfort soup with tender beef, potato chunks, and dried mushrooms is one of Tenzin Choenyi's favorite items on the menu. Of course, they make a homemade beef stock by letting beef, beef bones, and onions cook at a low heat—the liquid from the beef and onions is coaxed out, which becomes the broth of the dish. To make a quick broth versus using store-bought, add these ingredients—along with the required water—to a pressure cooker. To dress this soup up with more vegetables, add slivers of turnips or diced carrots when the potatoes are thrown into the soup. In Tibetan cooking, Tenzin says the use of peppercorn Sichuan began as a way to reduce any danger of food poisoning. The fireworks of tingling spice are just an added benefit to the Sichuan addition. Recipe adapted from Tenzin and Lobsang.

- 2 (½-ounce) packages dried mushrooms, like wood ear or shiitake
- 1 tablespoon canola oil
- 1½ pounds beef chuck pieces, cut into bite-size chunks
- 4 cloves garlic, minced
- 1 inch ginger, peeled and minced
- 1 teaspoon ground cumin
- 1 teaspoon ground turmeric
- ½ teaspoon ground coriander
- ½ teaspoon ground Sichuan peppercorns (optional)
- ½ teaspoon kosher salt
- 10 cups homemade or store-bought beef stock
- 1 pound baby potatoes, cut into bite-size pieces
- 6 ounces dried rice vermicelli noodles
- Chopped scallions, to serve
- Chopped cilantro, to serve

In a small bowl, add dried mushrooms and cover with hot water. Let sit 15 to 20 minutes.

In a large pot, warm oil over medium-high heat. Add beef pieces and cook until brown, just a few minutes per side. Stir in garlic, ginger, and spices, stirring to combine. Add enough beef stock to barely cover the meat. Bring to a boil, cover, and then reduce to low so the mixture is simmering. By this time, the mushrooms should be tender; add into the soup. Let cook until beef is tender, about 1 hour, depending on the size of the beef chunks. Taste broth, adjusting seasonings and salt as needed. When the meat is tender, add the potatoes, also cooking until tender, about 10 minutes.

Prior to serving, prepare the vermicelli noodles according to package instructions, usually by placing in a medium bowl covered with hot water for 10 minutes. To serve, add noodles into the serving bowls and ladle soup over it. Garnish with scallions and cilantro.

Substitution: 1 (8-ounce) package of baby bella mushrooms can be substituted for the dried mushrooms; just add into the soup along with the potatoes.

FOOD SHOP: Patel Brothers

I have a theory that many of those wacky ingredients stumping contestants on the Food Network's show *Chopped* have been hand-selected from this Southeast Asian grocer, mostly because I'll come across such items like bitter melon, raw sugarcane, green mango, fresh chickpeas, fresh turmeric, and jackfruit—and these are only observations from produce I can identify. If you ever find yourself in need of unusual food or vegetables (at a thrifty price to boot), Patel Brothers is what you're looking for. Their produce department offers a glimpse into another world, one with numerous fruits and vegetables unknown to many of us, and always gives me a thrill.

Produce at Patel Brothers. *(photo by Janis Turk)*

For years, Patel Brothers has remained a little-known place in Queens to grab essentials like lower-priced nuts, dried fruits, and ethnic condiments. The store says that the popular items are the staples—rice, beans, and their vast spice selections. Purchase a curry blend or make your own version using the fresh whole or ground spice options. I also always fill my basket with a jar of ghee, the clarified butter called for in many Indian recipes, a chutney or jar of pickled vegetables, mango nectar, and naan. All this I can usually get for under twenty dollars, at least half of what I pay at spice superstore Kalustyan's in Manhattan.

PATEL BROTHERS

Info: 37-27 74th St., Jackson Heights; 718-898-3445; patelbrothersusa.com

See You There: From Manhattan, take the R/M or the E/F subway into Queens, getting off at the Roosevelt Avenue-Jackson Avenue exit. Walk north on 74th St. to arrive at Patel Brothers.

Produce at Patel Brothers. *(photo by Janis Turk)*

Jackson Heights Walking Tour

Take the 7 train to the 74th Street/Broadway stop or the E/F/M/R to the Roosevelt Avenue-Jackson Heights stop. Find the 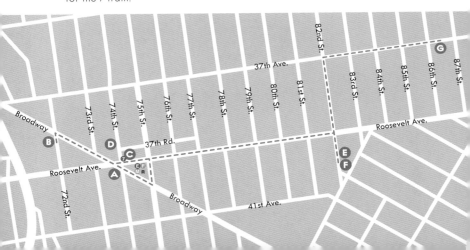**Tamales y Elote Cart** on Roosevelt and 74 Street. The selection of tamales can include mole, salsa verde, jalapeño-cheese; but really, just go for what's not sold out. Plenty of times I've swung by with a tamale craving, and they've been all gone by noon. Then head northwest on Broadway two blocks to one of Jeff Orlick's and Joe DiStefano's favorites: **Ⓑ Dhaulagiri Kitchen** (37-38 72nd St.). Sit down for a veggie thali plate while watching the ladies at Tawa Food in the back go about their daily roti-making duties, and purchase a few Tawa Food goods to go. Walk back on Broadway to 74th Street, make a left and walk one short block to 37th Road for the cash-only **Ⓒ Phayul** (37-65 74th St.; 718-424-1869). Trek up the flight of stairs and through a curtain to get into the restaurant. Watch the chef's wok-tossing abilities and share a table with strangers for any menu-ordering advice (the waitstaff also offers valuable info when asked). Split an order of Shoko Sil Sil Ngoe Ma (shredded potatoes with green peppers) and one of the best versions of the Himalayan blood sausages, Gyuma Ngoe Ma. Back on 74th street, make a right and go to **Ⓓ Tibet Mobile** (37-50 74th St.). Walk through the cell phone store to Lhasa Fast Food for the best momos in Jackson Heights (and probably all of NYC). Walk back to make a left onto Roosevelt Avenue and continue to 82nd Street (Note: if it's in the evening, check for the Arepa Lady on Roosevelt Ave. and 79th St.). Make a right onto 82nd Street for any Mexican goods at **Ⓔ Casa Rivera** (40-15 82nd St.; 718-426-7590) or a peek at the landmark **Ⓕ Jackson Heights Cinema** (40-31 82nd St.; 718-205-5100). Head back north on 82nd Street, walk 1½ blocks to 37th Avenue and make a right. Walk 4½ blocks to **Ⓖ La Nueva Bakery** (86-10 37th Ave.; 718-507-4785) for Uruguayan arrollados, much raved about by Noshwalks tour guide Myra Alperson. Make a right on 87th Street, walk back to Roosevelt Avenue. Make a left and continue to 90 St/Elmhurst Avenue station for the 7 train.

QUEENS FOOD PRO: Jeff Orlick, Jackson Heights food guide

What made you move to Queens and how long have you lived here? For the food! Seriously, I definitely lucked out. When I was deciding on where to live, it was between Greenpoint, Fort Greene, and Jackson Heights. Any one of them would have been good, but Jackson Heights won because I had a family friend who owned the building, and I got in easily. I would have had a totally different path had I wound up in either of the two other neighborhoods.

When I first moved here, it was quite intimidating with the amount of action happening at all times. I knew there was some Indian stuff, and some Mexican stuff, and I was aware of the Asian contingent in Elmhurst, but I really had no idea how much there really was.

What's your Queens claim to food fame? People know me for my events like Viva la Comida and Woks & Lox. People know my large-scale food crawls like the Momo Crawl and the Roosevelt Avenue Taco Crawls. Some know my pizza app, Real Pizza of New York, but most recently, people know my Roosevelt Avenue Midnight Street Food Crawl and the Ambassador Program. My friend James Boo calls me Mr. Roosevelt Avenue, but most others know me as Jeffrey Tastes, the Queens Qustodian or JeffSayYes. This area has so many possibilities, I can't help but keep busy.

What's your advice for going into a restaurant/food shop/etc. where you don't speak the language? Go in with someone from that culture. If you are alone, take your time and see what other people are getting. If it's your first time; things will be awkward. Don't be discouraged; come back again and again. If you really want to break in, you will. [Author note: Jeff also has given me excellent advice to ask people walking by to translate, something that has worked wonders for me once I started taking his advice for this book.]

What do you think is the biggest misconception about Queens? That it's far away. I have tourists come to me all the time, commuting from Manhattan, and they can't believe how quick the train ride is. Taking the F or E train from Midtown will take you all of twenty minutes to get to Roosevelt Avenue.

What's the most surprising experience (foodwise) you've had in Queens? Finding out people's careers before they opened a restaurant. You have doctors, professors, lawyers [from other countries] who cannot practice in the United States and no one will hire them; they have no choice but to open up their own business. My barber was a gynecologist in Russia—I think I can trust him with my hair.

Any favorite Queens memories? I am just so proud to be invited into the homes of some of the street vendors I've met. Hanging out in Tortas Neza's backyard with his family on Father's Day. Tacos la Familia's Laura and her husband, Victor, showing me the guinea pig shed in their backyard and watching them prepare her famous pancita for the night's vending. Being a guest in the homes of street vendors in Corona has shown me such a vision of my past and our future.

Describe your ideal eating day in Queens: I am so lucky to be able to satisfy just about any culinary want, all in the borough of Queens. And if I can't find it here, I can get it within forty minutes of travel time. That's why my favorite thing to do is lose control and get lost in someone else's world. It'd be a dream come true to hang out with a Nepalese family in my neighborhood, chill out, and eat what they eat for the whole day. Just enjoying flavors has a very short-term value to me—expanding my mind and meeting new friends is much more rewarding.

What type of non-food activities do you like to do in Queens or do you recommend others to do? I'm now a regular at LIC Flea; I love to walk around and see the commerce happening. Forest Avenue is one of the nicest parks, with the most diverse number of activities in the five boroughs.

Is there a string of restaurants that you constantly recommend to others and, if so, what are they? For the past couple of years, I have been telling people to check out the Tibetan and Nepalese restaurants in Jackson Heights. It's such a burgeoning community, all locally owned. The groups and individuals here are so creative and expressive—you really have to take notice of what is happening. How big is it? Within a square mile of the 74th Street station, there are twenty places where you can get the Himalayan dumplings called momos!

Name something you've only been able to find in a specific Queens location: Momo carts at 73rd Street and Broadway; there are three of them.

What are a few under-the-radar food places in Queens? Nearly everything but SriPraPhai, Fu Run, and M. Wells is under the radar. For a food writer, this place is an organic content farm.

Any Queens restaurant, food shop, truck, etc. that closed down for which you're still in mourning? Too many to mention. Food vending is a hard business and I do not envy anyone who begins to feed people as employment. Some of the street food ladies I miss, like Laura of Tacos la Familia, Maria Luna the tamale lady, and Maria the pupusa lady (she was so much more than that to me!).

Let's say you had to move out of the country: What would be your last meal in Queens? What food establishment would you miss the most? I'd love a nice, warm bowl of fresh-shaved beef noodle soup (thenthuk) from Tibet Mobile. It's such a comforting meal, and the people are the nicest, while the language barrier provides some privacy so I can sulk and not be bothered. One specific place I would miss is Tortas Neza. I would always wonder what type of trouble he's into now, and I'd miss his lengua tacos.

Any specific dishes from Queens restaurants that you've always wanted to make at home? I prefer to cook simply at home, leave the masterful complex renditions to the people with the equipment, time, know-how, and desire to do so. Something I'd like to know is what's in the pandebonos at Las Delicia de Pandebono for the simple reason that it is a closely guarded secret, and I love contraband.

What is your favorite...

Thai restaurant in Queens: In life, you have to make choices. Just about every Thai restaurant east of Sunnyside is great, but going to a different one every time would never establish a foundation for learning. Thai Center Point is the Thai restaurant I can most often be found in and where I always bring my friends. Annie Phim and her family are such nice, interesting people—creative and emotional. I always enjoy being with them and eating what's on the board this week.

Chinese restaurant in Queens: I love the scene of the New World Mall, but if you want one specific place, let's say Little Pepper in Whitestone.

Pizza in Queens: Amore in Flushing, but I love the women of John's in Elmhurst.

Dim sum in Queens: My girlfriend's parents always bring me to Jade Asian.

Greek in Queens: I would love to have an intelligent response to this, but I eat Greek food about once per year in New York City. You can't be everywhere at once.

Mexican in Queens: Maravillas Restaurant. It's a Mexican Karaoke bar with some very talented patrons.

Street cart in Queens: Tortas Neza

Dessert/bakery in Queens: Rio de la Plata, the Argentine bakery on Corona Avenue; everything is so precious there.

Other: I love JoJu's Vietnamese sandwiches. I am addicted to Casa del Pollo. And I am intrigued by Nick's Gourmet Deli in Astoria Heights—could their pastrami be the best in Queens?

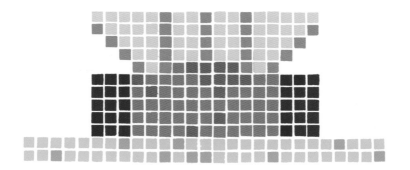

Fried fish balls at a storefront stand in Flushing.
(photo by Andrea Lynn)

FLUSHING

The roots of Flushing were established by English settlers in the mid-1600s, which you'll see when you walk by **St. George's Church** on 38th Avenue, which has been a religious and historical fixture in Flushing for three hundred years. But in recent decades, Flushing has been established as an Asian epicenter of New York City, one of the fastest-growing Chinese areas in the nation and always one of my favorite places to explore because I feel practically transported to another country.

Formidable Chinese cookbook author Grace Young gave me a heads up, telling me I'd never be able to get recipes in Flushing. But I was optimistic, thinking I could just get a couple of ingredients, which ended up being far from the case. Even with a translator, I had no luck getting anyone to spill any information about a dish. The answers were creative, though, with many shaking their heads and feigning absolutely no knowledge of anything, in fact. Even simple questions were brushed off, like when I asked if there's butter in the egg tart crust: "Even if the chef was here, he wouldn't tell you," was the response from several bakeries. The closest I got to any type of intel was from a cook at **Chengdu Heavenly Plenty Snacks** in **Golden Shopping Mall's** downstairs (page 000), who said some of their flavor combinations included "sweet, sour and numbing spice," but that was all he could say.

Flushing is a haven for Asian food-lovers, with mouthwatering options everywhere you turn. Pick up crispy scallion pancakes and roasted-duck-filled buns to snack on while exploring the streets and shops. Indulge in dumplings galore at **White Bear** or the multiflavored Taiwanese-style shaved ice at **S&C Shaved Ice** inside **Flushing Mall's Food Court**, opting for the multiflavored mango special. Come back on a weekend morning with a group of friends and head to **Jade Asian** for dim sum, where you'll feast on chicken feet, lotus–leaf wrapped sticky rice, and every imaginable type of dumpling.

Hunan Kitchen of Grand Sichuan

Chen Gangyi, owner and chef of the restaurant, said (through a translator) that a few components are the hallmark of Hunan cooking: sourness, spiciness, oiliness, and the right flavor. It's that harmonious balance that shines through the dishes. Take the Dan Dan Noodles, for example, a favorite pick of the non-Asian sect of restaurant goers. Noodles sit in a pool of sauce, seemingly simple yet radiating a numbing spiciness from Sichuan peppercorns, a shiny slick from chile oil, and a slightly tart yet umami quality that is hard to pinpoint. It culminates into an addictiveness that's hard to deny or understand.

Another reason for the uniqueness of the food, according to Chen (which may perhaps account for what is hard to pinpoint), is that ingredients like bamboo, spices, and more are imported straight from Hunan for a more authentic food experience. There's the Garlic and Cumin Pork Ribs made more pungently cumin by the Chinese-originated spice, the authentically Asian white pepper used for the White Pepper Smoked Beef or the special, high-secret chile peppers that the restaurant utilizes for pickling and chile oil steeping.

To navigate the menu, forget about the Chinese options and go straight for the Hunan recipes and distinctions. "Famous Hunan Dishes" designate, well, favorite dishes from the Hunan Province, the top picks being Boiled Sliced Fish in Hot Chile Sauce and Garlic & Cumin Pork Ribs. "Hunan Country-Style" refers to dishes that farmers would covet, like the much-ordered Sautéed Pork Stomach with Smoked Bamboo or the Sautéed Pork Farmer-Style. And "Old-Style Dishes" such as the White Pepper Smoked Beef and Sliced Cured Pork with Dry Strings Beans or Dry Turnips evoke memories of an older generation.

It's been the publicity, especially a *New York Times* review—which is also on the back page of each menu—that Gangyi says has attributed to the success of the restaurant, which has been operating for about five years. It's because of this good welfare that Hunan Kitchen has introduced a menu special of the Wang Wang Pot, brimming with pig's feet, pig's hock, Hunan-imported rice, and broad rice noodles. My translator explained that because "wang wang" sounds like a cheer and means prosperity, the dish signifies the restaurant's good fortune and thankfulness, and passes this goodwill on to the customer.

**Dan Dan Noodles at Hunan Kitchen of Grand Sichuan
before being mixed with sauce.** *(photo by Andrea Lynn)*

Dan Dan Noodles
Yield: 4 servings

This recipe is inspired by the Dan Dan Noodles at Hunan Kitchen,
which is a slurpy, Sichuan peppercorn-tingling delicious mess.
There's an umami quality about Hunan Kitchen's noodles that I had a
hard time pinpointing, and the kitchen was pretty mum on ingredients.
So this is a less-complicated spin to get a taste of Sichuan Dan Dan
Noodles at home.

Sichuan peppercorns are usually sold in their full form (and for good quality, try kalustyans.com). Toast the peppercorns in a dry sauté pan over high heat until aromatic, about 1 minute. Then use a food processor or a spice grinder to grind the peppercorns. If you can't find Chinese noodles, substitute with 16 ounces of fettuccini noodles. Recipe inspired by Hunan Kitchen of Grand Sichuan.

1 (16-ounce) bag Chinese plain, thick noodles
    (fresh preferred, but dry works, too)
1 (10-ounce) container sliced baby bella mushrooms,
    finely chopped
1 (5-ounce) container fresh baby spinach
1 cup chicken stock
½ teaspoon instant bonito dashi (optional)
3 tablespoons ground bean paste
2 tablespoons soy sauce
2 tablespoons balsamic vinegar
1½ tablespoons chile oil
1 tablespoon sesame oil
1 teaspoon granulated sugar
1½ to 2 teaspoons ground Sichuan peppercorns
    (depending on desired spiciness)
2 teaspoons cornstarch

Bring a large pot of water to a boil over high heat. Add noodles and mushrooms, cooking noodles according to package instructions (usually around the 5 minute or less mark). One minute before noodles are done, add spinach to the pot, stirring to let combine and wilt entirely. Drain noodles and vegetables in a colander, and transfer to a large serving bowl.

Meanwhile, in a medium bowl, add the remaining ingredients, except for the cornstarch. In a large pot (you can reuse the pot the noodles boiled in for ease), add the sauce ingredients. Bring to a boil over high heat, stirring to combine.

Make a slurry with the cornstarch: add cornstarch to a small bowl along with a few tablespoons of the sauce mixture from the pot. Stir to combine with a spoon. Add this cornstarch slurry back into the pot, whisking to combine. Let mixture boil just 1 to 2 minutes until slightly thickened. Remove sauce from heat and pour over noodles. Serve with tongs and a spoon, the better to stir the noodles and distribute the sauce when serving.

Dumplings from Tianjin Dumpling House at Golden Shopping Mall. *(photo by Andrea Lynn)*

Golden Shopping Mall

There are a few food malls in Flushing, but I fondly refer to Golden Mall as the "crazy mall," due to the layout of the space, which can be completely overwhelming if you don't know how to navigate it. But I've laid out a plan for walking through the space. To begin, go straight to the bottom floor, which came to fame by Anthony Bourdain eating his way through the stalls.

- **Chengdu Heavenly Plenty Snacks:** The first stall upon entering this underground wonderland boasts a display with various types of Sichuan cold salads to choose from. One worth mentioning is the common cucumber salad, except with the crispier Persian cucumber swimming in chile oil. There's also a salad of smoked tofu strands and the house special salad, which is a combination of glass noodles, carrot shreds, and sea kelp, along with pork ears and chicken feet. A popular dish among the Chinese is the Xo Tongue and Tripe (loosely translated into tongue and tripe in a spicy sauce); the man at the counter said non-Asians go for the Dan Dan noodles or Cheng Du cold noodles. There are also photos of dishes for easier menu choosing, and you can nab tables across from the counter for easyseating.

- **Tianjin Dumpling House:** Walk straight past Chengdu; at the corner of a left turn toward more stalls is Tianjin. *Serious Eats* editor Max Falkowitz told me that hands-down the best dumplings are in Flushing, particularly the lamb dumplings from Tianjin. The lady behind the counter swore the sea bass fish dumplings were the most popular, but sitting down with a plate, the lady next to me spoke her hesitations about that recommendation. A biweekly visitor to the stall, she said most Chinese eaters order the pork dumplings, especially the pork dumplings with dill, but added that the powerful dill could be too much for some. The pork dumplings with cabbage are the most likely to be made in Chinese homes for Chinese New Year, similar to how a Thanksgiving dinner celebrates the togetherness of cooking and eating as a family. Pour the Chinese black vinegar over the dumplings and dot with spoonfuls of chile oil to eat.

- **Xi'an Famous Foods:** Next to Tianjin is the first location of Xi'an that brought adoration for Xi'an Famous Foods, now with other locations throughout Manhattan, and a sister store, Biang!, in Flushing. Their claim to Flushing food fame is their Stir-Fried Liang Pi Cold Skin Noodles and the Spicy Lamb Burger, of which Anthony Bourdain remarked, "It's this lamb burger that hits me right in the pleasure zone." Unlike the bigger-is-better American version of a sandwich, these small, flattened sandwiches pack a wallop of taste. And the same bread used for the lamb burger is diced to make the Lamb Pao-Mo Soup. Named after Xi'an, the capital of the Shaanxi Province in China, the prevalence of lamb on the menu is meant to appeal to the large, non-pork-eating Muslim sector of that population.

- **Lanzhou Handmade Noodles:** Right across from Xi'an Famous Foods, you can get a lesson in hand-pulled noodle making. The cook at Lanzhou Handmade Noodles slaps the dough against the metal table with a large thud (said to wake up the dough) and then does magical handiwork with a maze of quick stretches and pulls in less than a minute. A native Chinese customer now based in City Island said she has to visit the food stall at least twice a month to put homesickness at bay; the Beef Pulled Noodle (number one on the menu) is as authentically Chinese as it gets.

Sichuan Cucumber Salad ■■■■■■■■■■
Yield: 4 servings ■■■■■■■■■■■■■■

This cold, crunchy cucumber salad is addictive. And there are various incarnations of it, a few of which are on display at the Golden Shopping Mall. Some, like Chengdu Heavenly, bathe the cucumbers in a spicy chile oil, while Tianjin Dumpling House prefers a less-saturated method of red hot chile flakes. This version is a compilation of a few different methods. While seedless Chinese cucumbers are used, they can be extremely difficult to find. (If you do find them, use about 5 to 6 for the recipe.) A close second are English/hothouse cucumbers, just because they have fewer seeds, which equals less liquid leaching out and diluting the spicy vinaigrette.

> 4 cups chopped cucumbers (about 2 English hothouse
>   cucumbers or 4 regular cucumbers)
> 1½ teaspoons kosher salt
> 1 tablespoon hot chile oil
> ½ tablespoon soy sauce
> 2 teaspoons rice vinegar
> 1 teaspoon sugar
> ½ teaspoon to 1 teaspoon red hot chile flakes
>   (depending on desired spiciness)
> ½ teaspoon ground Sichuan peppercorn (optional)

Use a peeler and peel every other horizontal row of each cucumber. (There's a reason for this besides also being pretty. In a marinated cucumber salad like this, the entire peel makes it too firm, but no peel makes the cucumber too soft. Keeping just half the skin is just right.) Lay cucumbers on a cutting board, and gently bash the cucumbers with a rolling pin or chef's knife until it has slightly broken down. (The thought process here is that bruising the cucumber makes it a flavor magnet for absorption.)

Then, cut the cucumber into 2-inch chunks. Place in a bowl, and stir in salt. Let cucumbers sit for a minimum of 30 minutes.

When the cucumber has sat 30 minutes, transfer to a colander and rinse off salt. Blot cucumbers dry with paper towels. In a small heat-proof bowl, add chile oil, soy sauce, rice vinegar, sugar, red hot chile flakes, and Sichuan peppercorns (optional). Briefly heat in the microwave, about 30 seconds, and stir to make sure the sugar is dissolved. Add cucumbers to a bowl, along with dressing, and mix to combine. Let cucumber salad refrigerate for a minimum of 30 minutes prior to serving.

FOOD SHOP: Assi Plaza

I daresay it doesn't get better than buying bags of kimchee that you've just watched expertly prepared, by ladies expertly massaging the cabbage with the chile mixture. That's a must on the to-buy list, along with the fresh tofu and soy milk at the front of the store (sometimes complete with samples). And if you've ever been in need of 5-pound bags of Korean red chiles, Assi Plaza is where you can get them. It's like a Korean-food Ikea, with a dumpling restaurant in the back of the store in case you've worked up an appetite while shopping. The produce manager says the bestselling items are Japanese condiments like sesame oil, soy sauce, and seaweed, so the supermarket doesn't just specialize in Korean goods. Wander through the incredible produce section for fresh water chestnuts, durian, and more, along with the fresh fish and seafood aisle.

ASSI PLAZA
Info: 13101 39th Ave, Flushing; 718-321-8000

See You There: Take the 7 train into Queens to the last stop (Flushing). Exit at the Main St. and Roosevelt Ave. exit; walk west on Roosevelt Ave., make a right onto College Point Blvd., and then a left onto 39th Ave. (about a 10-minute walk from the subway).

Freshwater chestnuts for the taking, (top)
and Kimchee being prepared at Assi Plaza.
(photos by Andrea Lynn)

Chung Fat Supermarket

Doesn't the name alone just make you want to do your Asian grocery shopping here? The truth is that Flushing has a plethora of Asian supermarkets, like **Hong Kong Supermarket, Jmart**, and **H Mart,** and each one offers its own set of perks and drawbacks. Chung Fat gets my vote for easy navigating as far as finding items. A few of the standouts include the spices, a majority of which come straight from Asia (check the back of the label to confirm). When interviewing restaurateurs in Flushing, some of the little bit of info I could gather was a belief that the spices direct from Asia are better and more potent. Also, if you're ever inclined to use MSG in your Asian cooking (much-loved by many Chinese cooks), you can get a giant bag at the supermarket. A jar of fried chiles adds crunchy heat to dishes, and I've found a spoonful or two of ground bean sauce harnesses an umami quality, like in the Dan Dan Noodles recipe on page 181. The fresh Asian noodles in the refrigerated section are also a must, along with bags of dumplings to stock the freezer. Along with most of the store in Flushing, freshness and prices in the grocery section and fish aisle are unparalleled—I try to grab as much as I can drag a few blocks back to the subway.

CHUNG FAT SUPERMARKET
Info: 41-82 Main St., Flushing; 718-886-9368

See You There: Take the 7 train into Queens to the last stop (Flushing). Exit at the Main St. and Roosevelt Ave. exit; walk south on Main St. to Chung Fat.

Maxin Bakery

The long (but incredibly quick) line takes over this tiny shop, which is always a good sign when looking for standouts. The challenge can be maneuvering the baked selections around the people waiting to check out. A few other locations around Flushing (135-24 40th Rd. and 3701 Main St.) are larger with sit-down options; this one is more grab-and-go as you get on or off the 7 train.

A variety of steamed buns is the first thing to encounter, which are offered sweet and savory options. These light, fluffy egg-based rolls are slightly sweetened; options include lemon, red bean, and what I discovered was my favorite: the rolls topped with pork threads. Sure, it sounds a little odd, but the crunchy, salty dehydrated pork strands match the fluffy sweetness of the bread. There is also a selection of circular pressed cakes with various fillings, referred to as "wife cakes." According to lore (and my translator), when husbands would go on long journeys, wives would make these flattened pastries for them to carry and eat along the way.

Traditionally, Chinese baked goods rely on natural fats like lard, since butter was viewed as a luxury item. And the flaky layers in these desserts might have you reaching for lard for all your baking needs. Maxin's egg custard tarts are on the less-sweet side, which I find preferable. Just a glance at an egg tart can lend insight into what you're buying. The yellowness of the custard indicates how eggy it is: Light yellow means it's milkier, and bright yellow means it's egg-heavy. Egg tarts like these have more of a pastrylike crust; the Portuguese egg custards that are also around Flushing have a phyllolike dough. And the dough color is a sign of its flakiness: Aim for perfectly golden. (Note: Egg tarts sit in two doughs pressed on top of each other, an oil dough and a water dough, which makes them challenging to replicate at home.)

MAXIN BAKERY
Info: 136-76 Roosevelt Ave. in Flushing; 718-762-2222
See You There: Take the 7 train to the Flushing stop. Bakery is right off the stop.

Egg custard tarts. *(photo by Andrea Lynn)*

Dehydrated Pork-Topped Pork Buns

Yield: about 20 to 24 rolls

Dehydrated pork sure sounds better than the usual translation of this Asian treat, which goes by the name of "meat floss" or "pork floss" and is available at Asian food markets or online at amazon.com. These sweet, fluffy rolls are topped with the salty, porky goodness of these flakes for a sweet-salty effect and an unexpected riff on the usual morning roll. Sweet yeast roll base adapted from *Bon Appétit*.

⅔ cup whole milk
5 tablespoons granulated sugar, divided
1 (¼-ounce) envelope active dry yeast
3 large eggs, at room temperature, divided
2¾ cups all-purpose flour
1 teaspoon kosher salt
½ cup (1 stick) unsalted butter, cut into 1-inch pieces
    at room temperature
Cooking spray or canola oil
2 tablespoons water
2 tablespoons mayonnaise
½ cup to 1 cup pork floss/dehydrated pork

In a small saucepot over medium heat, warm milk until it registers a heat of 110° to 115°F. Transfer milk to a small, heatproof container and stir in 1 tablespoon sugar. Sprinkle the yeast over milk and whisk to combine. Add 2 eggs, whisking again to combine.

In the bowl of a food processor, add remaining 4 tablespoons sugar, flour, and salt. Pulse to blend. Add milk mixture and process to combine. Then, with the food processor running, through the feed tube add butter, one slice at a time, blending well between additions. Process until dough is soft and pillowy, about 1 to 2 more minutes. Dough should be sticky. If it's greasy, keep processing for 1 to 2 more minutes. Coat a medium-size bowl with cooking spray or canola oil. Transfer dough to the prepared bowl. Cover tightly with plastic wrap. Let dough rise in a warm area until it has doubled in size, about 2 hours.

Line a baking sheet with foil and coat with cooking spray. Pull off pieces of dough (as evenly as you can) and roll/shape each one into a ball. Make 20 to 24 rolls, evenly spaced out on baking sheet, so they are almost touching. Loosely cover with plastic wrap, and let the dough rise until doubled again, 1 to 2 hours.

When the rolls have risen, preheat the oven to 425°F. Grease 2 (9-inch) cake pans with cooking spray. Place the dough on a flour-dusted cutting board. In a small bowl, whisk together remaining egg and water. Use a brush to gloss the egg wash over each roll. Cook in preheated oven until rolls are browned, about 12 to 15 minutes.

When the rolls have cooled, spread a thin layer of mayonnaise over all of the rolls. Then, spread a layer of dehydrated pork on the top. Use your hands to lightly press down so the dehydrated pork adheres to the roll. Serve.

Jade Asian Restaurant

Cantonese in custom, "dim sum" refers to snacks that were offered to accompany tea sipping. Centuries later, the term has reversed itself in notion; think of dim sum as Asian small plates popular for a weekend brunch. After years spent dim summing in Chinatown, I switched to Flushing, finally settling on dim sum at Jade Asian. Their steam baskets are filled beyond the normal dumpling options and provide an overall more authentic eating experience.

As you'll see below in my guide to tackling dim sum, expect to chase down carts for the food you want. Also, cart-rollers will assume newbies only want dumplings, and will insist on those options for you. Be firm, and ask them to raise the lid on all the steamer baskets to see everything.

Jade Asian Restaurant's fried head-on shrimp at dim sum. *(photo by Andrea Lynn)*

Remember that dim sum is better enjoyed with a crowd—if simply because the more people you have, the more you can order and share. My Jade Asian favorites include the weblike puffiness of taro dumplings, the thick lotus leaves filled with sticky rice and meat, shrimp-stuffed sweetened eggplant, and the head-on fried shrimp (which are meant to be crunched through the shells to eat, with the shells then spit out). Other more common yet still tasty dim sum delights are slick piles of thick white rice noodles rolled with meat inside with a quick pour of soy sauce over it, and the ever-popular steamed pork–bun.

Navigating Dim Sum

- Both *Serious Eats* and *BuzzFeed* (reprinted from *Lucky Peach*) offer Essential Guides to Dim Sum. They are worth scrolling through prior to any dim sum adventure. The guides match up photos with the food descriptions, making navigating through dim sum options easier.

- The busier, the better. Sure, there are crowds to fight for dishes and a line to wait in before being seated, but that's when you're sure to have the most variety of dim sum treats, along with freshness.

- It took many, many trips to Jade Asian Restaurant before I got the idea that there is an English dim sum sheet you can ask for at the cashier. Unlike the other one, you can see the English name of what you're grabbing. This can help as far as knowing what you like and what to order at other dim sum restaurants. Oh, and you'll also have a clearer knowledge of what you're eating when in doubt.

- Also, if you have a choice of seating, go for tables around the exit of the kitchen: those dim sum offerings will be piping hot.

- Extras like ice water or hot sauce need to be asked for. If you know you'll be in need, nicely request it as soon as you sit down versus trying to find your waiter throughout service, which can be a difficult process.

- Etiquette states that the youngest person at the table should pour tea for everyone else, along with making sure to keep everyone's tea cups full throughout the meal. Need more tea? Position the lid of the teapot at an angle on the top to signal a refill.

- It's okay to get up and chase down a cart for a dish you want and, personally, I find that part of the dim sum experience charming. It's not often you have to run after your food, and it's almost a game of sorts. When you see dessert items, grab them immediately. That cart may not roll around for the duration of your meal, and your need for a sweet fix at the end might not be fulfilled.

- Look around and see what other tables are getting; viewing and mimicking is the hallmark of any truly authentic food experience. The baskets are relatively cheap; if there's something you don't like, it's not a substantial loss.

- If the table is getting too crowded with dishes, place your chopsticks in a criss-cross design over a basket to signify that the table is finished with it.

- Take the receipt to the cash register in the front to pay, but make sure to leave a cash tip at the table, too.

> **JADE ASIAN RESTAURANT**
> **Address:** 136-28 39th Ave., Flushing; 718-762-8821;
> jadeasianrestaurant.com
>
> **See You There:** Take the 7 train into Queens to the last stop (Flushing). Exit at the Main St. and Roosevelt Ave. exit; walk north on Main St. to 39th Ave. Make a right onto 39th Ave. and the restaurant will be close (and huge! You can't miss it.). *Dim sum is only available for lunch.*

Fang Gourmet Tea

I mentioned to Max Falkowitz another impending research food trek around Flushing, where he said Fang Gourmet Tea was a must-stop. I'm a tea fan, so why not? Set in a small mall-style building on Roosevelt Avenue, Fang Gourmet Tea doesn't just sell tea—it's out to elevate the knowledge of the tea drinker. It was a tea ceremony that prompted Theresa Wong to trade in her stressful job in insurance sales to work at Fang Gourmet. "I got into tea not just for the taste but the relaxation," says Wong. She comes across as one of the calmest people ever, no small feat for someone who works in the caffeine industry.

Tea is filtered into large categories: green teas, black teas, and the vast in-between referred to as oolong. Because of this, tasting specific leaf-types versus going on type of blend is a more productive way to buy tea. Arrive on a less-busy day for the shop or during the weekend, when at least one of their two tables isn't occupied by tea drinkers, and you can be treated to a tasting to determine your favorites before purchasing. In fact, Theresa would prefer that you list your least-favorite types of tea, so she can find one within that realm to blow your tea-loving mind. The tea ceremony uses a porcelain gaiwan, a lidded vessel that allows the tea leaves to simultaneously brew and steam. Theresa's tea excitement is infectious, and you'll be tempted to walk out of the store with as much China- or Taiwain-exported tea and tea gear that you can afford and carry.

Because certain phrases in describing the nuances of tea don't translate from Chinese to English, Theresa use winelike descriptions to better convey the messages to non-Chinese-speaking tea clients, as they've had an influx of them over the years. In some ways the non-Chinese clientele are more open-minded, realizing how little they knew about tea when they walk into the shop versus many Chinese customers, who may think they are tea experts and can't be swayed to try new things, according to Theresa. Also, she stressed that tea drinking is more about relaxation and less about caring if the water is a perfect temperature or how many tea leaves to use for a cup.

Tea-tasting at Fang Gourmet Tea.
(photo by Andrea Lynn)

Tea Insights

- Like wine, tea can also be aged to mellow out the flavor; just place in a bag versus an air-tight container for storage.

- Always keep tea in a clean environment, as it absorbs moisture from the air around it. Theresa says that's one of the reasons that supermarket tea fails. There are just too many flavors around for them to soak up.

- Sniffing a tea before purchasing or brewing isn't going to tell you anything. Hot water is needed to release the taste, so nothing can be determined until brewing it.

- Wong steeps her tea leaves for just around 1 minute and says most people are oversteeping their tea by doing it longer than that. Also, tea leaves can be reused within the same day, with most teas, like oolong, registering 5 to 8 reuses and green tea a little fewer than 5.

- A sign of a good batch of tea is when you can look into your cup of tea and see the bottom of the cup: "Bright but not cloudy," as Theresa says.

- Don't throw away used tea leaves. Theresa advises using them for composting or mixing with dried lavender for a potpourri of sorts.

FANG GOURMET TEA
Info: 135-25 Roosevelt Ave. in Flushing; 888-888-0216; tea also available online via fangtea.com
See You there: Take the 7 train to the last stop, Flushing/Main St.; the shop is right off the stop.

Soy Bean Chen Flower Shop

Joe DiStefano alerted me to this wondrous tofu on one of his Flushing food tours. I instantly fell in love and always start a visit to Flushing with a stop at the shop. Who knew I could love tofu? But this proves the distinct difference between homemade and store-bought.

Around for two decades and open seven days a week from 8:30 a.m. until 9 p.m., it's easy to see just the greenery of the flower shop and zone out about the take-out window in the front. For a couple of bucks, Chen or his wife will scoop out the silkiest, creamiest tofu known to mankind. (Okay, or maybe just to me.) The sweet version has a ginger-spiked simple syrup from rock sugar that you pour over the warm soybean curd. The savory selection (called "saline beancurd"

Fresh tofu with ginger simple syrup at Soy Bean Chen Flower Shop. *(photo by Andrea Lynn)*

on the menu) is a Sichuan-version of this breakfast treat topped with a quite pungent combination of dried shrimp, pickles, and chiles. The peanut with bean curd offers the sweet syrup spiked with peanuts. (To find a place to enjoy your tofu, just make a left out of the store, a left onto Prince Street, and walk to Bland Playground—yes, that's its real name—to nab a bench.)

There's also tea eggs (halved and plopped into ramen noodles or eaten for breakfast), steamed buns, and the more rare yan ball. The yan balls are sold as a bag for five dollars, meant to take home and cook in soup. Similar to wontons in wonton soup, the skin of the yan balls are made from "beaten pork" (which constitutes beating and flattening a piece of pork) versus the more popular Shanghai-version of using flour dough. She says no matter how hard you boil them, these Fujian Province treats are made so they won't break during cooking. Grab extra tofu for upcoming breakfasts along with fresh soy milk and a bag of yan ball dumplings to boil in broth for lunch or dinner.

SOY BEAN CHEN FLOWER SHOP
Info: 135-26 Roosevelt Ave. in Flushing; 718-352-3232
See You There: Take the 7 train to the last stop, Flushing/Main St.

Fu Run

Cumin- and Chile-Coated Breast of Lamb
Yield: 3 to 4 servings

You'd never know it from the twenty-something-dollar price tag on the entrée, but I was nicely surprised to learn that breast of lamb is actually a completely reasonably priced purchase, especially in comparison to other ribs. Fu Run braises the lamb until tender; then it's topped with the cumin seed-heavy spice rub. At the restaurant, the lamb is deep-fried to make the fat on it crunch and the spice mixture crispy. This is nearly impossible in the home kitchen, so the fryer method has been swapped out for a quick stint in a blazing hot oven instead. The jar of fried red chiles is available in Asian food markets. Also, note that due to the richness of the lamb, it's hard to pinpoint the serving size. If making for a crowd, it's best to double to make sure you have enough on hand. Recipe inspired by Fu Run.

1 (about 3-pound) breast of lamb
8 cloves garlic
2 bay leaves
3 tablespoons whole cumin seeds, divided
½ tablespoon whole black peppercorns
Kosher salt, as needed
2 tablespoons whole black sesame seeds
2 tablespoons whole white sesame seeds
3 tablespoons jarred minced fried chiles or 2 tablespoons
    red hot chile flakes plus 1 tablespoon canola oil

Use a knife to trim as much visible fat from the lamb as possible. Depending on the size of your Dutch oven, you may need to use kitchen shears to divide the lamb in half to fit the pan. Add lamb to the Dutch oven, filling with enough water to cover completely. Add garlic, bay leaves, 1 tablespoon cumin seeds, and salt. Bring to a boil over high heat; when boiling, cover and reduce to a simmer. Cook until tender—but still on the bone—about 1½ to 2 hours. Remove from heat and let the lamb cool in the cooking liquid. (From this point, lamb can be refrigerated in cooking liquid until needed.)

When ready to serve, preheat oven to 500°F. (If the lamb has been refrigerated, let it come to room temperature before cooking, about 45 minutes.) In a medium skillet, add remaining 2 tablespoons cumin seeds and black and white sesame seeds, stirring until seeds are toasted and fragrant, about 2 to 3 minutes (careful not to burn). Transfer seeds to a small bowl and combine with the minced, fried chiles (or chile flakes and oil). Add lamb to a foil-lined baking sheet. Use a spoon or your hands to coat the top of the lamb with the spice coating. Place in the oven (away from direct fire, on the lower level of the oven, if necessary) and cook until lamb is warmed, careful to make sure the topping doesn't burn. Remove from oven, and serve.

Fu Run's famous Muslim Lamb. *(photo by Andrea Lynn)*

Rambutan.
$4.99 LB

A box of rambutan on the Flushing streets. *(photo by Andrea Lynn)*

Duck buns at Corner 28 in Flushing. *(photo by Andrea Lynn)*

Flushing Walking Tour

Equipped with cash, take the 7 train into Queens to the last stop, Main Street-Flushing. Exit at the corner of Roosevelt Avenue and Main Street. Walk 1 block southwest on Roosevelt Avenue and make a right on Prince Street. At **Ⓐ Fu Run** (40-09 Prince St., 718-321-1363), take a seat to split the much-raved-about (and rightly so) Muslim Lamb. A breast of lamb is first braised and then fried with a crunchy cumin/sesame-seed and chile-pepper coating. Turn back to the corner of Prince Street and Roosevelt Avenue for **Ⓑ White Bear** (135-02 Roosevelt Ave.), a hole-in-the-wall famous for its hot-chile-oil-slathered wontons, but you're welcome to try other dumpling options, too. Next, check out the deli counter next door at **Tian-Jin** (also B, 135-02 Roosevelt Ave.). The semi-exotic selection is quite extensive: snails, pig's feet, pig ears, tripe, cow liver, rabbit, duck necks. As far as the most popular, the shop says it's their par-boiled and smoked chicken and pig's feet that draw in the most sales. Everything smells distinctly of Chinese five-spice powder with a tilt toward star anise. As I let a woman go ahead of me while I mulled over the options, she told me I'd regret that deed after seeing how much she had to order: "This is like going to Costco. You bring it home, heat it up, and are ready to go."

Continue a block south on Prince Street and make a left on 40th Road. Walk one block back to Main Street to **Ⓒ Corner 28** (40-28 Main St.; 718-886-6628) for the super-cheap and super-delicious Cantonese-style Peking

Duck Buns. Next, walk 1½ blocks south on Main Street to ⓓ **Biang!** (41-10 Main St.; 718-888-7713) and slurp your way through the Liang Pi "Cold Skin" Noodles, along with the Lotus Root Salad. Backtrack 1 block and cross to the other side of Main Street to find the ⓔ **Xinjiang BBQ Cart** at the intersection of Kissena Boulevard and 41st Avenue and grab their famous lamb skewers before heading a half block on Kissena to ⓕ **Kung Fu Tea** (41-11 Kissena Blvd.; 718-886-6836) to sip your way through some bubble tea. For bubble tea addicts, find the chewy tapioca balls called boba at any Asian supermarket (see page 000) to make your own bubble tea: boil ¼ cup boba for 5 to 10 minutes until soft and then plop into iced tea with milk or Vietnamese coffee. Head back to Main Street and past the subway station. If you have any remaining stomach space (which is doubtful), take an 8-minute detour, continuing on Main Street, making a right on Northern Boulevard, and then a quick left onto Farrington Street to ⓖ **Mamak House** (35-20 Farrington St.; 718-886-4828), which *Saveur* editor-in-chief James Oseland said was the "best Malaysian food in the States right now," specifically citing their shrimp curry with fresh turmeric leaves; the crispy okra is another must-try. Return back to the 7 train to head home.

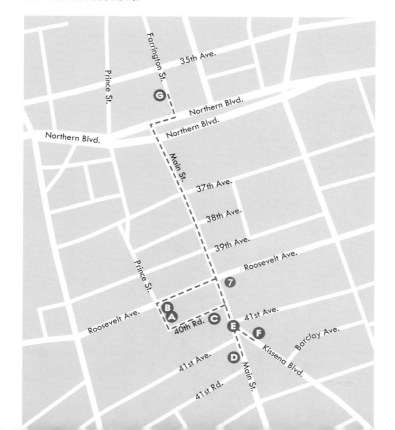

QUEENS FOOD PRO: Joe DiStefano, Queens food guide and blogger at *Chopsticks and Marrow*

What made you move to Queens and how long have you lived here? At the time I was living with a girlfriend in Staten Island. We broke up and I moved to Woodside and then Rego Park where I currently reside. All told, I have lived in Queens for fifteen years.

Name the reasons you love Queens: Food, culture, a real sense of neighborhood and community. And the 7 train!

What's your Queens claim to food fame? Well, I used to think it was turning Anthony Bourdain on to the lamb face salad at Xi'an Famous Foods, or taking Fuchsia Dunlop to Golden Shopping Mall, but hands down I'd have to say curating the Queens episode of Bizarre Foods America and spending a day shooting with Andrew Zimmern.

What's the most surprising experience you've had in Queens? It's a tie between eating roasted guinea pig—delicious—at someone's house and the streetside Bangladeshi chaat in Jackson Heights.

Any favorite Queens memories? The year they held the Vendys by the Unisphere was pretty awesome. Also eating every sandwich from Tortas Neza with some friends was an epic undertaking.

Describe your ideal eating day in Queens: Early a.m. breakfast of kari laksa at Curry Leaves in Flushing with as many add-ins as possible, a steam at Spa Castle, lunch at M. Wells Dinette, late Nepalese dinner at Dhaulagiri Kitchen in Elmhurst.

What type of non-food activities do you like to do in Queens or do you recommend others do? There are non-food activities? A visit to the Louis Armstrong House. Walk through Corona Park to sit by the Unisphere and check out the Queens Museum of Art. A visit to the Thai Buddhist temple in Elmhurst. A visit to the Ganesh Temple in Flushing.

Is there a string of restaurants that you constantly recommend to others and, if so, what are they? Phayul, M. Wells Dinette, Salt & Fat, Fu Run, Lao Dong Bei, Lao Cheng Du, La Fusta

Name something you've only been able to find in a specific Queens location: The amazing guo tie, pork and leek dumplings with "wings" at Li's Noodles in New World Mall.

What are a few under-the-radar food places in Queens? Lhasa Fast Food in the back of the Tibet Mobile cell phone store in Jackson Heights, Soy Bean Chen Flower Shop on Roosevelt Avenue in Flushing, and La Esquina de Camaron Mexicano on Roosevelt and 80th for freshly made Mexican shrimp cocktails.

Any specific dishes from Queens restaurants that you've always wanted to make at home? I love the turkey/lamb shawarma at Grill Point—not sure how I'd make it at home. A recipe I'd like to get is the hot sauce from Wafa's. It's something of a running joke between me and her son, Yusef.

What is your favorite...

Italian restaurant in Queens: Cucina a Moda Mio. They're from Calabria like my mom's family. It's the non-mobsters' answer to Park Side.

Thai restaurant in Queens: Zabb Elee; love all their Isaan-style dishes, plus it is open late.

Chinese restaurant in Queens: Fu Run for its Muslim lamb chop, cumin fish, tiger vegetables, bean sheet jelly, really everything.

Pizza in Queens: John's on Grand Avenue. It's like 1965 preserved in amber in there.

Dim sum in Queens: A tie between Jade and Grand for great variety and freshness.

Greek in Queens: BZ Grill for Greek fries with feta and oregano and killer pork gyros.

Mexican in Queens: Tortas Neza for his oversized sandwiches.

Street cart in Queens: The Arepa Lady, she's an institution.

Dessert/bakery in Queens: Cannelle

Specialty food spot: Tortilleria Nixtamal

Other: Dhaulagiri Kitchen for amazing Nepali food!

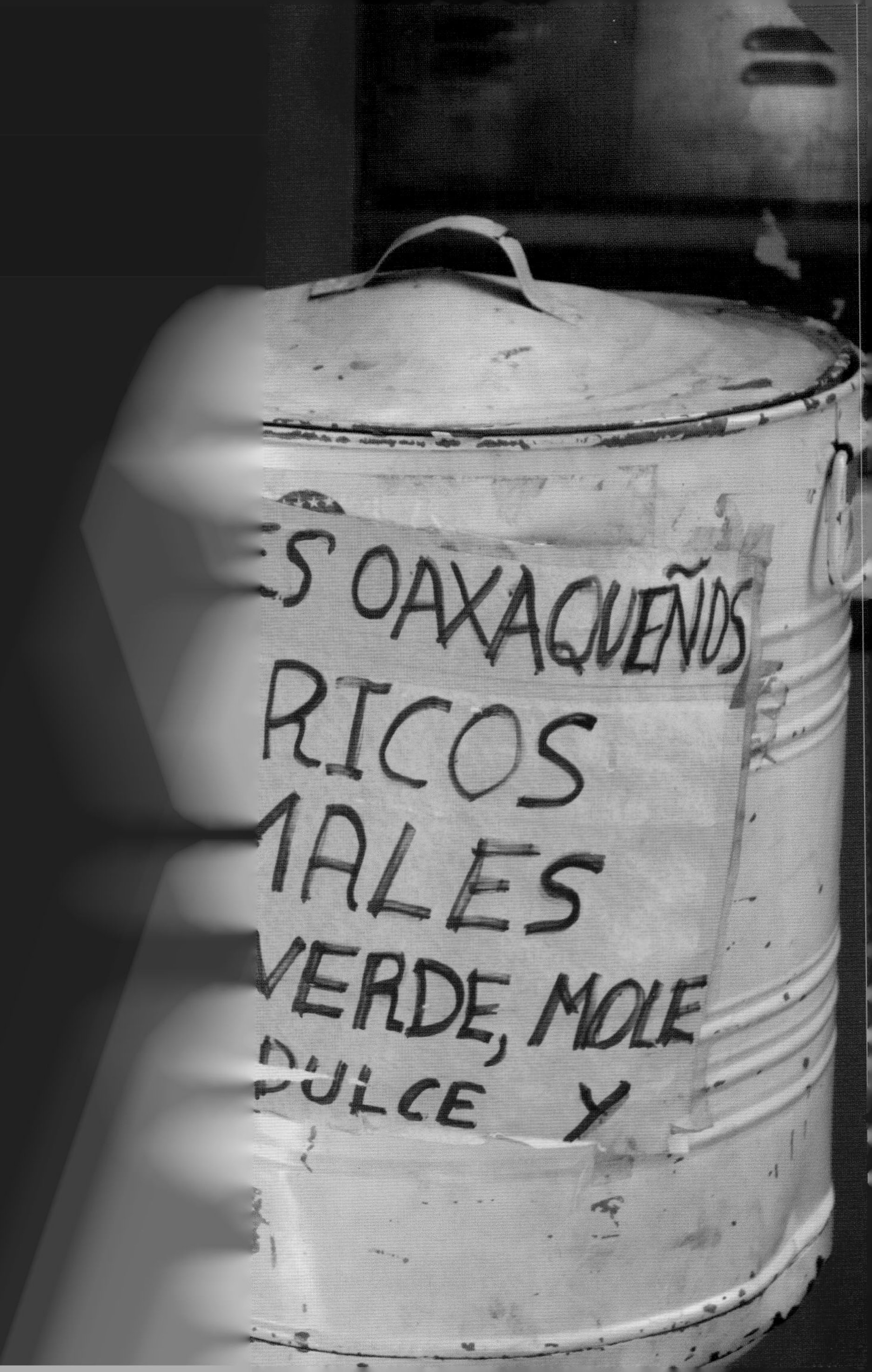
S OAXAQUEÑOS
RICOS
MALES
VERDE, MOLE
DULCE Y

ACKNOWLEDGMENTS

Food writers in Queens are a generous bunch, eager to share anything and everything to make their borough shine. I am grateful to all those who were always happy to field questions, recommend restaurants, and put me in touch with others: Max Falkowitz, Katrina Schultz Richter, Lesley Tellez, Alia Akkam, Jeff Orlick, Joe DiStefano, Meg Cotner, Famous Fat Dave, and Myra Alperson.

Kudos to my husband, Ryan, who was willingly dragged to so many restaurants, and who critiqued the recipes as I was recipe testing them, as well as a handful of recipe testers who double-checked the recipes for me.

Without Jean Sagendorph and St. Martin's Press there would be no book, and thanks to Courtney Littler for edits, suggestions, and input. I'm especially grateful to jack of all trades, Cristina Alonso, for all the help she offered in research, restaurant calling, photo shoot—accompanying, fact-checking, and more. And to my food writing partner-in-crime, Casey Barber, who always gave support. Also, thanks to Janis Turk, who graciously aided in photography.

Thanks to Seth Bornstein and Rob MacKay of the Queens Development Economic Council for all the work they do to promote the borough and the feedback they gave in the beginning, especially their kindness when I showed up in their office on the day of what turned out to be Hurricane Sandy aftermath.

And, of course, thanks to all the restaurants in Queens, that took a break from their hectic schedules to graciously answer questions, give me recipes, and generally share a little piece of their life with me. It's their hard work and dedication that help make this unique borough what it is.

INDEX

achiote, 81
Acosta, Rudy, 79-81, 83
Adobong Manok (Chicken Adobo), 124-26
Afelia (Red Wine Pork), 12-13
Albenio, Mario, 124, 126
Albenio, Nenette, 124-25
Aloo Dum (Sho-Go Khatsa), 158, 160-61
Alperson, Myra, 89-91, 172
Alpha Donuts, 94-95
American food, 141
    Kale Salad with Almonds, Anchovy Dressing, and Parmesan, 38-39
    Mac and Cheese, 23, 31, 36-38, 40
    Sea Scallops with Truffled Corn Salsa and Roasted Carrot Purée, 98-99
    in Sunnyside, 95, 97-101
    Three-Alarm Buffalo Chili, 130-31
    see also Quebeco-American food
anchovies, 144
    Kale Salad with Almonds, Anchovy Dressing, and Parmesan, 38-39
André's Hungarian Bakery, 46-47, 64
Angelis, Nick, 64
Apollo Bakery, 24
Arepa Lady, The (Maria Piedad Cano), 25, 155, 172, 203
Argentinian food, 88, 90, 112, 175
arrollados, 90-91, 172
Arroz con Pollo, 79, 81-83
Asians, Asian food, 38, 62-63, 89
    in Elmhurst, 91, 98, 112, 138-45, 149, 151, 173, 202
    in Flushing, 66, 91, 111-12, 151, 179-203
    in Sunnyside, 95, 97, 100-101, 106-10
    in Woodside, 24, 117-28, 132-33, 135
Assi Plaza, 186-87
Astoria, 1-25, 89, 111, 135, 151, 175
    Cypriot food in, 11-14, 23
    food shops in, 3-4, 19, 22-23, 60
    Greek food in, 2-11, 15-21, 23-25, 91, 111-12
    Italian food in, 3, 22-24
    Mexican food in, 25, 72, 112
    Middle Eastern food in, 3, 15, 66-67, 112
    walking tour of, 22-23
Athens Café, 2-4
avocados, 24, 36, 73, 78, 119
    Avocado Shake, 125, 128
    Mexican-Style Seafood Cocktail, 145-48
Ayada Thai, 91, 112, 139, 143-44

Baba Rum, 23
Baby Jesus Cake, 24-25
bakeries, 25, 88-91, 113, 149, 203
    in Astoria, 3, 23, 89, 91
    in Corona, 77, 88, 175
    in Flushing, 24, 179, 188-91
    in Forest Hills/Rego Park, 46-47, 64
    in Jackson Heights, 172
    in Woodside, 24, 91, 117-19
Bambino, Il, 24
Bangladeshi food, 164, 202
banh mis, 161
    Lemongrass Chicken Banh Mi, 140-43
Barbacoa Lamb Tacos, 75-76
barbecue, barbecue sauce, 66, 75, 90, 117-19, 141, 201
    Korean Barbecue Lettuce Wraps with Marinated Steak and Pickled Vegetables, 100-101
    LA Galbi, 107, 109-10
Barragan, Santiago, 72-73, 75-76
Bay Gull, 66
beef, 20, 48-49, 59, 62, 66, 71, 73, 95, 103-7, 117, 130, 141, 149-50, 156-59, 164, 166, 174, 180-81, 184, 200
    LA Galbi, 107, 109-10
    Lasagna, 71, 85-87
    Liver and Onions, 33-34
    Mole de Olla (Beef and Chile Broth), 150
    Phingsha (Beef Soup with Potatoes), 158, 166, 169-70
    Shabhaley (Tibetan-Style Empanadas), 167-68
    Shepherd's Pie, 103-4, 117
    see also steaks, steak
Ben's Best Kosher Deli, 47-53, 66

Biang!, 151, 184, 201
Bizarre Foods America, 202
Bletsas, Frideriki, 16, 18
Bletsas, Gregory, 16, 19
boba, 201
Bourdain, Anthony, 3, 15, 66, 117, 183-84, 202
branzino, 6, 8
breads, 25, 36, 48, 132-33, 141, 158, 164, 184, 189
  pita, 19-20, 60
  soda, 101, 117
  torta, 71, 77-79
  Tsoureki, 19
  see also buns; sandwiches
Bruni, Frank, 120
Budweiser Beer, 79-83
buns, 188-92, 196
  Dehydrated Pork-Topped Pork Buns, 189-91
  duck, 179, 200-201
  egg-based, 188-91
burgers, 23, 66, 97, 117, 128, 133, 184
Butcher Block, 101-4
butchers, 23, 34, 88, 109
  in Sunnyside, 101-4
  in Woodside, 114, 128-31
BZ Grill, 112, 135, 203

Cabana, La, 25, 135
cabbage, 64, 95, 106, 184, 186
  Stuffed Cabbage with Tomato-Raisin Sauce, 49-51
Cactus, Orange, and Pineapple Juice, 148-49
Café Boulis, 23
Café du Monde, 141, 145
Café Nueva, 90
calamari, 6, 24, 123, 146
Cannelle Patisserie, 113, 203
cannolis, 23, 25, 71, 85
carrots, 24-25, 52, 112, 141, 143, 156, 169, 184
  Sea Scallops with Truffled Corn Salsa and Roasted
  Carrot Purée, 98-99
Casa America, 90
Casa Enrique, 41, 112
Casa Rivera, 172
Cedars Meat House, 22, 112
Chak Chak, 63
Chami, Wafa, 58-61
Chang, David, 66, 117
Chao Thai, 98, 112, 135, 138-39
Chao Thai Too, 139, 151
Cheburechnaya, 62-63
cheese, 32, 59, 105, 172
  feta, 7, 16, 18-19, 24, 203
  Filipino Pimento Cheese, 132-33
  Gouda, 22, 24
  Greek Salad, 6-8, 81
  Kale Salad with Almonds, Anchovy Dressing, and
  Parmesan, 38-39
  Lasagna, 71, 85-87
  Mac and Cheese, 23, 31, 36-38, 40
  mozzarella, 3, 22, 25, 64, 71, 85-87
  Parmesan, 22-23, 38-39
  ricotta, 85-87
  Spicy Greek Cheese Dip (Tirokafteri), 18-19

Cheese of the World, 64
Cheley, 157
Chen Gangyi, 180
Chengdu Heavenly Plenty Snacks, 179, 184-85
chicken, 6, 10, 20, 38, 52, 72, 77-78, 113, 123,
  151, 160-64, 179, 184, 200
  Arroz con Pollo, 79, 81-83
  Chicken Adobo (Adobong Manok), 124-26
  chopped liver and, 49
  fried, 97-98, 133
  Lemongrass Chicken Banh Mi, 140-43
  Peruvian Roasted Chicken with Aji Verde (Green
  Sauce), 135, 161-64
  Poussin au Pot, 28, 34-35
  Torta de Milanesa (Mexican-Style Breaded
  Chicken Cutlet), 78-79
chickpeas, 85-86, 170
  King of Falafel's Famous Falafel, 20-21
Chilean food, 89, 91
chiles, 98, 117, 125, 149, 164, 180-81, 188, 196,
  200
  Cumin- and Chile-Coated Breast of Lamb, 197-98
  Mole de Olla (Beef and Chile Broth), 150
  Salsa Roja, 73-74
  Shrimp Enchiladas (Enchiladas Camerones), 76-77
  Shrimp with Thai Chile Sauce, 143-44
  Szechuan Cucumber Salad, 184-86
  Three-Alarm Buffalo Chili, 130-31
China, Chinese food, 62-63, 125, 135, 156, 166,
  175
  Cumin- and Chile-Coated Breast of Lamb, 197-98
  Dan Dan Noodles, 180-82, 184, 188
  Dehydrated Pork-Topped Pork Buns, 189-91
  in Elmhurst, 139, 149, 151
  in Flushing, 24-25, 91, 111-12, 151, 179-203
  Szechuan Cucumber Salad, 184-86
  teas and, 111, 191-94, 201
chocolate, 25, 32, 101
  Egg Cream, 47, 54, 56-57
Choenyi, Tenzin, 165-69
Choephel, Lobsang, 166-67, 169
Chung Fat Supermarket, 188
Cienaga Grocery and Deli, 88
Citrano, Vito, 54, 57
coffee, 3-4, 22, 90
  Vietnamese, 141, 145, 201
Colombia, Colombian food, 91, 95, 136
Confiteria Buenos Aires, 90
corn, 71-73, 91
  Sea Scallops with Truffled Corn Salsa and Roasted
  Carrot Purée, 98-99
Corner 28, 200-201
Corona, 68-91, 133, 174-75
  Cuban food in, 25, 79-85
  desserts in, 68, 71, 81, 88, 135
  Ecuadorian food in, 89-90
  Italian food in, 71, 85-88, 112
  Mexican food in, 70-79, 88-89, 91
  walking tour of, 88
Cotner, Meg, 24-25
crabs, 98, 120, 144
Cuban food:
  Arroz con Pollo, 79, 81-83

in Corona, 25, 79-85
  Ropa Vieja, 25, 81, 83-85
Cucina a Moda Mio, 203
cucumbers, 36, 106, 141, 156
  Szechuan Cucumber Salad, 184-86
curries, 25, 120, 135, 139, 171, 201
Cypriot food:
  in Astoria, 11-14, 23
  Cypriot Pork Sausage (Sheftalia), 11, 14, 23
  Red Wine Pork (Afelia) with Cracked Wheat Pilaf
  (Pourgouri), 12-13
Czech food, 24, 32

Dan Dan Noodles, 180-82, 184, 188
DeBenedittis, Marie, 71
Delicia de Pandebono, Las, 175
Dhaulagiri Kitchen, 172, 202-3
dim sum, 112, 175
  in Flushing, 179, 191-93, 203
dips, 25, 61, 77, 105, 108, 112, 144
  Spicy Greek Cheese Dip (Tirokafteri), 18-19
DiStefano, Joe, 172, 195, 202-3
Donovan's Pub, 66, 117
donuts, 94-95
  Sour-Cream Drenched Donuts (Papanasi), 95,
  104-6
Dorado Café, El, 90-91
Drunken Noodles, 120-21
duck, 132, 181
  buns, 179, 200-201
Dufour, Hugue, 32-33
dumplings, 32, 62, 66, 90, 135, 156, 165-66, 174
  in Flushing, 111-12, 179, 183-84, 188, 191-92,
  196, 200, 202
Dutch Kills, 41

East Ocean Palace, 112
Ecuadorians, Ecuadorian food, 151
  in Corona, 89-90
  in Jackson Heights, 155
  in Sunnyside, 91, 95
Eddie's Sweet Shop, 44, 47, 53-59, 111
Egg Cream, 47, 54, 56-57
eggplant, 22-23, 105, 151, 192
eggs, 77, 95, 106, 125, 135, 141
  buns and, 188-91
  tarts and, 179, 189
Egyptian food, 3, 15, 66-67, 112
Elmhurst, 89, 136-51
  Asian food in, 91, 98, 112, 138-45, 149, 151,
  173, 202
  Chinese food in, 139, 149, 151
  food shops in, 139, 142, 144-46, 148-49
  Indonesian food in, 139, 149
  Italian food in, 175
  Mexican food in, 145-50
  Nepalese food in, 202
  Thai food in, 91, 98, 112, 138-39, 143-44, 149,
  151
  Vietnamese food in, 139-45, 149
  walking tour of, 149
Elmhurst Mex Grocery Company, 148-49
empanadas, 62, 133, 135

Shabhaley (Tibetan-Style Empanadas),167-68
enchiladas, 72-73
  Shrimp Enchiladas (Enchiladas Camerones), 76-77
  epazote, 75
Ephron, Nora, 64
Esquina del Camaron Mexicano, La, 145-48, 202

falafel, 19-22, 111, 113
  King of Falafel's Famous Falafel, 20-21
Falkowitz, Max, viii, 110-13, 184, 193
Famous Fat Dave, 65-67
Fang Gourmet Tea, 111-12, 193-95
Fieri, Guy, 31, 36, 80-81
Filipinos, Filipino food, 90, 119-20, 132-35
  Avocado Shake, 125, 128
  Chicken Adobo (Adobong Manok), 124-26
  Filipino Pimento Cheese, 132-33
  Oxtail Stew in Peanut Butter Sauce (Kare Kare),
  126-27
  in Woodside, 119, 124-28, 132-33, 135
Finkelstein, Larry, 5
fish, 6, 11, 67, 101, 106, 116-17, 149, 180-81,
  186, 188, 203
  Broiled Whole Fish with Oregano and Lemon, 8-9
  fried, 16, 116, 120, 132, 135, 144, 178
  see also specific kinds of fish
5Pointz, 42-43
Flushing, 89, 133, 135, 149, 162, 175-203
  bakeries in, 24, 179, 188-91
  Chinese food in, 24-25, 91, 111-12, 151, 179-
  203
  food shops in, 91, 186-88
  Indian food in, 111
  Italian food in, 175
  Japanese food in, 186
  Korean food in, 66, 186-87
  walking tour of, 200-201
food shops, 24, 112-14, 170-74, 197
  in Astoria, 3-4, 19, 22-23, 60
  in Corona, 88
  in Elmhurst, 139, 142, 144-46, 148-49
  in Flushing, 91, 186-88
  in Forest Hills/Rego Park, 64, 90
  in Jackson Heights, 123, 160, 164, 170-72
  in LIC, 31-32, 35-40
  in Sunnyside, 101-4
  in Woodside, 114, 116, 119, 124, 128-33, 135
Forest Hills/Rego Park, 24, 44-67, 110, 112, 133,
  135, 161, 202
  bakeries in, 46-47, 64
  food shops in, 64, 90
  Hungarian food in, 46-47, 64
  Jewish food in, 47-53, 62-63, 66, 89-90
  Middle Eastern food in, 58-62
  Russian food in, 62-63
  sodas in, 44, 47, 53-58
  walking tour of, 64
Freddy, 113
French food, 31, 41, 141
Fu Run, 112, 174, 197-98, 200, 202-3

Ganesh Temple Canteen, 111, 202
Gauchito, El, 88, 111

Gaynor, Noel, 101-3
Georgiou, George, 11
Gian Piero Bakery, 3, 23
Golden Palace, 24-25
Golden Shopping Mall, 91, 112, 179, 183-86, 202
GoogaMooga Celebration, 32
Greeks, Greek food, 135, 175
  in Astoria, 2-11, 15-21, 23-25, 91, 111-12
  Broiled Whole Fish with Oregano and Lemon, 8-9
  Greek Frappé, 3-4
  Greek Lemon Roasted Potatoes, 9-10, 100
  Greek Salad, 6-8, 81
  Grilled or Broiled Octopus, 6, 16-18, 24
  King of Falafel's Famous Falafel, 20-21
  Shawarma, 20, 112-13, 203
  Spicy Greek Cheese Dip (Tirokafteri), 18-19
green sauces, 25, 141
  Peruvian Roasted Chicken with Aji Verde (Green Sauce), 135, 161-64
Gregory's 26 Corner Taverna, 3, 15-19, 24-25, 112
Grill 43, 111-12
Grill Point, 203
Guli, La, 25
Gurung, Gyaltsen, 156-58, 160
gyuma (Tibetan sausage), 156-57, 166, 172

Haab, The, 24
halo-halo, 119, 125, 132
Himalayan food, 155-61, 166, 172, 174
Himalayan Yak, 155-61
Hirachan, Ranjit, 107
Hong Kong Supermarket, 139, 188
Hostess cupcakes, 31, 35-38
Humba, 125
hummus, 22, 59, 67
Hunan Kitchen of Grand Sichuan, 180-82, 203
Hungarian food, 25
  in Forest Hills/Rego Park, 46-47, 64
  in LIC, 32

ice cream, 53-55, 111, 125
  Ice Cream Soda, 54-55, 57-58
  Ice Cream Sundaes, 47, 54-55
Ikan Pepes, 149
India, Indian food, 135, 166
  in Flushing, 111
  in Jackson Heights, 155-57, 164, 171, 173
Indonesian food, viii, 139, 149
International Meat Market, 23
Irish food, 66
  Shepherd's Pie, 103-4, 117
  in Sunnyside, 101-4
Italian food, 25, 38, 101, 203
  in Astoria, 3, 22-24
  in Corona, 71, 85-88, 112
  in Elmhurst, 175
  in Flushing, 175
  Lasagna, 71, 85-87

Jackson Diner, 155
Jackson Heights, 24-25, 89-90, 152-75
  Ecuadorian food in, 155

food shops in, 123, 160, 164, 170-72
  Himalayan food in, 155-61, 166, 172, 174
  Indian food in, 155-57, 164, 171, 173
  Mexican food in, 25, 172-73
  Nepalese food in, 155-56, 172, 174, 202-3
  Pakistani food in, 164-65
  Peruvian food in, 161-64
  Thai food in, 119, 135
  Tibetan food in, 154-61, 165-70, 172, 174, 202
  walking tour of, 172
Jade Asian Restaurant, 175, 179, 191-93, 203
jam, 22, 47, 101-2
  Sour-Cream Drenched Donuts (Papanasi), 95, 104-6
Jewish food, 155
  in Forest Hills/Rego Park, 47-53, 62-63, 66, 89-90
  Latkes (Potato Pancakes), 49, 51-52, 135
  Matzo Balls, 34, 47, 49, 52-53
  Stuffed Cabbage with Tomato-Raisin Sauce, 49-51
Joe's Pizza, 91
Joe's Shanghai, 135
John Brown Smokehouse, 41
John's, 175, 203
JoJu Modern Vietnamese Sandwiches, 139-44, 161, 175

Kabab Café, 3, 15, 66-67
Kababish, 164-65
Kabir's, 135
Kale Salad with Almonds, Anchovy Dressing, and Parmesan, 38-39
Kalustyan's, 171, 182
Kare Kare (Oxtail Stew in Peanut Butter Sauce), 126-27
kibbeh, 59
kimchee, 22, 97, 106-9, 141, 186-87
  Korean-Style Kimchee Pancakes, 107-8, 113
King of Falafel and Shawarma, 19-21, 111-12
knishes, 48, 64, 67, 135
Knish Nosh, 64-65, 67, 135
Kopiaste Taverna, 11-14
Korean food, 90, 133, 141
  in Astoria, 22
  in Flushing, 66, 186-87
  Korean Barbecue Lettuce Wraps with Marinated Steak and Pickled Vegetables, 100-101
  Korean-Style Kimchee Pancakes, 107-8, 113
  LA Galbi, 107, 109-10
  in Sunnyside, 95, 97, 100-101, 106-10
  in Woodside, 117
Krystal's, 24, 135
Kung Fu Tea, 201

LA Galbi, 107, 109-10
lamb, 15-16, 19-20, 32, 59, 62, 67, 111-14, 135, 164, 184, 200-203
  Barbacoa Lamb Tacos, 75-76
  Cumin- and Chile-Coated Breast of Lamb, 197-98
  Muslim Lamb, 198, 200, 203
  Shepherd's Pie, 103-4, 111
Lanzhou Handmade Noodle, 91, 184
Laphing (mung jelly), 156-57

Lasagna, 71, 85-87
Latkes (Potato Pancakes), 49, 51-52, 135
Laucella, Rosa, 85-86
Lebanese food, 22, 112
  in Forest Hills/Rego Park, 58-62
lemon, 68, 77, 88, 188-89
  Broiled Whole Fish with Oregano and Lemon, 8-9
  Greek Lemon Roasted Potatoes, 9-10, 100
Lemongrass Chicken Banh Mi, 140-43
Lemon Ice King of Corona, The, 68, 71, 88-89, 135
lentils, 85-86, 111-12
  Mujadarah, 59-62
Leo's Latticini, 71, 88
lettuce, 73, 78, 163
  Greek Salad, 6-8, 81
  Korean Barbecue Lettuce Wraps with Marinated
Steak and Pickled Vegetables, 100-101
Lhasa Fast Food, 172, 202
LIC Flea & Food, 41, 174
LIC Market, 135
Little Tibet, 155, 165-70
liver, 49, 200
  Liver and Onions, 33-34
Long Island City (LIC), 24, 26-43
  American food in, 31, 35-40
  food shops in, 31-32, 35-40
  French food in, 31, 41
  graffiti at 5Pointz in, 42-43
  Mexican food in, 41, 112
  Pepsi-Cola sign in, 26-27, 31
  Quebeco-American food in, 28, 31-35
  walking tour of, 41
Louis Armstrong House, 90, 202

Mac and Cheese, 23, 31, 36-38, 40
Mahankali, Arvind, 49
Malaysian food, 201
Mamak House, 201
Mama's, 71, 88
mangos, 119, 144, 164, 170-71, 179
  Shredded Green Mango Salad, 122-24
Maravillas Restaurant, 175
Marjolaine, La, 91
Matzo Balls, 34, 47, 49, 52-53
Maxin Bakery, 188-91
mayonnaise, 36, 141
Mexican food, 83, 151, 172-75, 202-3
  in Astoria, 25, 72, 112
  Barbacoa Lamb Tacos, 75-76
  Cactus, Orange, and Pineapple Juice, 148-49
  in Corona, 70-79, 88-89, 91
  in Elmhurst, 145-50
  in Jackson Heights, 25, 172-73
  in LIC, 41, 112
  Mexican-Style Seafood Cocktail, 145-48
  Mole de Olla (Beef and Chile Broth), 150
  Salsa Roja, 73-74
  Shrimp Enchiladas (Enchiladas Camerones), 76-77
  Torta de Milanesa (Mexican-Style Breaded
Chicken Cutlet), 78-79
  in Woodside, 119
Mexican-French fusion dishes, 41
mezzes, 11, 15, 111

Okra and Tomato Mezze, 59-61
Middle Eastern food, 111-12
  in Astoria, 3, 15, 66-67, 112
  in Forest Hills/Rego Park, 58-62
  Okra and Tomato Mezze, 59-61
Mishan, Ligaya, 139
MitchMallows, 41
moles, 72-73, 88, 172
  Mole de Olla (Beef and Chile Broth), 150
Molinero, Galdino, 70, 77-79
Mombar, 15
Momofuku, 31, 66, 117
momos, 90, 133, 156-57, 166, 172-74
Monterey Vegetable Sandwich, 36
Morscher's Pork Store, 91
Mujadarah, 59-62
Mundo, 24, 112
Muslim Lamb, 198, 200, 203
M. Wells Dinette, 28, 30-35, 174, 202

Natural Tofu Restaurant, 95, 106-10, 113
Nepalese food, 89-90, 166
  in Elmhurst, 202
  in Jackson Heights, 155-56, 172, 174, 202-3
New World Mall, 91, 175, 202
Nick's Gourmet Deli, 175
Nick's Pizza, 64, 112
Nilsson, Leslie, 35-38
noodles, 25, 62-63, 119-21, 125-26, 135, 149,
151, 174, 192, 196, 201
  Dan Dan Noodles, 180-82, 184, 188
  Drunken Noodles, 120-21
  Lasagna, 71, 85-87
  Mac and Cheese, 31, 36-38, 40
  Phingsha (Beef Soup with Potatoes), 158, 166,
169-70
Nueva Bakery, La, 172
nuts, 25, 63, 171
  Kale Salad with Almonds, Anchovy Dressing, and
Parmesan, 38-39
  see also peanuts, peanut butter

Obama, Michelle, 36
Obraitis, Sarah, 32-33
octopus, 3, 19, 25, 66, 91, 117
  Grilled or Broiled Octopus, 6, 16-18, 24
  Mexican-Style Seafood Cocktail, 145-48
Okra and Tomato Mezze, 59-61
Ongee Crab, 98
onions, 11, 25, 36, 51, 77-78, 101, 145, 156, 169
  Greek Salad, 6-8, 81
  Liver and Onions, 33-34
  Mujadarah, 59-62
oranges, 22, 81, 155
  Cactus, Orange, and Pineapple Juice, 148-49
Orlick, Jeff, 155, 172-75
Oseland, James, 201
Ottomanelli, Mike, 128
Ottomanelli & Son's Prime Meat Shop, 114, 128-31
oxtail, 81
  Oxtail Stew in Peanut Butter Sauce (Kare Kare),
126-27
  terrine, 97-98

Pad Kra Prao with Crispy Pork, 138
Pad Thai, 119-20
Page, Shauna, 72
Pakistan, Pakistani food, 156
   in Jackson Heights, 164-65
pancakes, 111, 117, 179
   Korean-Style Kimchee Pancakes, 107-8, 113
   Latkes (Potato Pancakes), 49, 51-52, 135
Panch Phoran, 160
Pancit Bam-I, 125
pandebonos, 175
Papanasi (Sour-Cream Drenched Donuts), 95, 104-6
Parker, Benjamin, 48-49
Parker, Jay, 48-49, 51-52
Park Side Restaurant, 71, 112, 203
Parrot Market, 25
Patel Brothers, 123, 160, 164, 170-71
peanuts, peanut butter, 144, 196
   Oxtail Stew in Peanut Butter Sauce (Kare Kare),
126-27
Peruvian food, 25, 141
   in Jackson Heights, 161-64
   Peruvian Roasted Chicken with Aji Verde (Green
Sauce), 135, 161-64
Phayul, 154-55, 172, 202
Phil-Am Foods, 116, 119, 124, 132-33, 135
Phim, Annie, 175
Phingsha (Beef Soup with Potatoes), 158, 166,
169-70
Pho Bang Restaurant, 139, 149
pies, 19, 25, 31, 59
   Shepherd's Pie, 103-4, 117
pineapples, 24, 54, 72, 132-33
   Cactus, Orange, and Pineapple Juice, 148-49
Pio Pio, 135, 141, 161-64
pizza, 22, 25, 38, 64, 66, 97, 112, 173, 175, 203
pork, 72, 98, 117, 125, 135, 138, 141, 151, 180-
81, 184, 188-92, 196, 200, 202-3
   Cypriot Pork Sausage (Sheftalia), 11, 14, 23
   Dehydrated Pork-Topped Pork Buns, 189-91
   Lasagna, 71, 85-87
   Red Wine Pork (Afelia) with Cracked Wheat Pilaf
(Pourgouri), 12-13
Portales, Los, 112
Portuguese, Portuguese food, 78, 89, 189
potatoes, 32, 64, 67, 101, 156, 172
   Greek Lemon Roasted Potatoes, 9-10, 100
   Latkes (Potato Pancakes), 49, 51-52, 135
   Phingsha (Beef Soup with Potatoes), 158, 166,
169-70
   Shepherd's Pie, 103-4, 117
   Sho-Go Khatsa (Aloo Dum), 158, 160-61
Pourgouri (Cracked Wheat Pilaf), 12-13, 100
Poussin au Pot, 28, 34-35
PS1, 30, 32-33
pupusas, 91, 174

Quebeco-American food:
   in LIC, 28, 31-35
   Liver and Onions, 33-34
   Poussin au Pot, 28, 34-35
Queens County Market, 133-34, 161

Queens Kickshaw, The, 22, 24

Rajbhog Sweets and Snacks, 155
rambutan, 199
raspberry linzer tarts, 46-47, 64
Red Ribbon, 119
red snapper, 149
Red Wine Pork (Afelia) with Cracked Wheat Pilaf
(Pourgouri), 12-13
Rego Park, see Forest Hill/Rego Park
Rendang Padang, 149
rice, 49, 98, 107-9, 111, 125-26, 132, 135, 144,
149, 156, 158, 171, 179-80, 192
   Arroz con Pollo, 79, 81-83
Richter, Katrina Schultz, 132-35, 161
Rincon Criollo, 25, 79-85
Rio de la Plata Bakery Shop, 88, 175
Rizzo's Fine Pizza, 22
Rodriguez, Pedro, 145-46
Rokhat Bakery, 64, 90
Romanian food, 90
   Sour-Cream Drenched Donuts (Papanasi), 95,
104-6
Romanian Garden, 95, 104-6
Roosevelt Grocery Corp., 145-46
Ropa Vieja, 25, 81, 83-85
Rose & Joe's, 25
Roussopoulos, Paraskevi, 12, 14
Ruiz, Fernando, 72
Russian food, 62-63

Sabry Restaurant, 91
Sage General Store, 31, 35-40
salads, 24-25, 78, 105, 117, 120, 139, 151, 156-
57, 201-2
   Greek Salad, 6-8, 81
   Kale Salad with Almonds, Anchovy Dressing, and
Parmesan, 38-39
   Shredded Green Mango Salad, 122-24
   Shrimp with Thai Chile Sauce, 143-44
   Szechuan Cucumber Salad, 184-86
salsas, 172
   Salsa Roja, 73-74
   Sea Scallops with Truffled Corn Salsa and Roasted
Carrot Purée, 98-99
Salt & Fat, 95-101, 139, 202
Salvadorans, Salvadoran food, 90-91
Samayabajee, 156-57
San Antonio bakery, 91
S&C Shaved Ice, 179
sandwiches, 24, 41, 184, 202-3
   with bagels, 66
   in Corona, 71, 77-79, 88
   eggplant Parmesan, 22-23
   fois gras-stuffed grilled cheese and horse bologna,
32
   Lemongrass Chicken Banh Mi, 140-43
   pastrami, 47-49
   roast-beef, 71
   steak, 36
   Torta de Milanesa (Mexican-Style Breaded
Chicken Cutlet), 78-79

sausages, 3, 22-23, 77, 101-2, 125
  Cypriot (Sheftalia), 11, 14, 23
  Filipino (longaniza), 119, 132, 135
  Romanian (mitten), 95, 105
  Tibetan (gyuma), 156-57, 166, 172
Sayed, Ali El, 3, 15, 66-67
scallops, 6
  Sea Scallops with Truffled Corn Salsa and Roasted
Carrot Purée, 98-99
sea bass, 6, 184
sea food, 3, 5, 66, 101, 107, 117, 120, 125-26,
132, 186, 191-92, 202
  Grilled or Broiled Octopus, 6, 16-18, 24
  Mexican-Style Seafood Cocktail, 145-48
  Sea Scallops with Truffled Corn Salsa and Roasted
Carrot Purée, 98-99
  Shrimp Enchiladas (Enchiladas Camerones), 76-77
  Shrimp with Thai Chile Sauce, 143-44
Shabhaley (Tibetan-Style Empanadas), 167-68
Shapta (Sautéed Sliced Beef), 157-59
Shawarma, 20, 112-13, 203
Sheftalia (Cypriot Pork Sausage), 11, 14, 23
Shepherd's Pie, 103-4, 117
Shi, 38
Sho-Go Khatsa (Aloo Dum), 158, 160-61
Shoko Sil Sil Ngoe Ma (Shredded Potatoes with
Green Peppers), 172
short ribs, 117
  LA Galbi, 107, 109-10
shrimp, 6, 120, 123, 125-26, 143-49, 191-92,
196, 201-2
  Mexican-Style Seafood Cocktail, 145-48
  paste, 126, 132, 135, 144, 149
  Shrimp Enchiladas (Enchiladas Camerones), 76-77
  Shrimp with Thai Chile Sauce, 143-44
Shun Wong, 151
Sifton, Sam, 31
Sik Gaek, 117
Sik Gaek Chun Ha, 66
Sincronizada, 72-73
Singh's Roti Shop, 25
sisig, 119, 125
Skenderi, Ardian, 6-8, 10, 19
Slovak Czech Varieties, 24, 32
Slovenian food, 91
smoothies, 128, 148-49
sodas, 47-49, 101, 119, 141
  Egg Cream, 47, 54, 56-57
  in Forest Hills/Rego Park, 44, 47, 53-58
  Ice Cream Soda, 54-55, 57-58
Sorriso Italian Pork Store, 3, 22-23
soups, 62-63, 105-7, 119-20, 125, 135, 149, 157,
165-66, 174, 184, 196
  Matzo Ball, 34, 47, 49, 52
  minestrone, 85-86
  Mole de Olla (Beef and Chile Broth), 150
  Phingsha (Beef Soup with Potatoes), 158, 166,
169-70
Sour-Cream Drenched Donuts (Papanasi), 95, 104-6
Soy Bean Chen Flower Shop, 195-96, 202
Spanish food, 83, 125
spices, 81, 128, 130

SriPraPhai, 25, 117-24, 174
Starry Bakery & Café, 149
steaks, steak, 33, 36, 88, 111, 128
  Korean Barbecue Lettuce Wraps with Marinated
Steak and Pickled Vegetables, 100-101
  Ropa Vieja, 25, 81, 83-85
  Shapta (Sautéed Sliced Beef), 157-59
stews, 11, 95, 106-7, 130
  Oxtail Stew in Peanut Butter Sauce (Kare Kare),
126-27
Stifado Kouneli, 11
Strawberry Ice Cream Soda, 55, 58
suadero, 112
sundubu, 95, 106-7
Sunnyside, 24, 89-113, 133, 151
  American food in, 95, 97-101
  butchers in, 101-4
  Ecuadoran food in, 91, 95
  food shops in, 101-4
  Irish food in, 101-4
  Korean food in, 95, 97, 100-101, 106-10
  Romanian food in, 95, 104-6
  sign in, 92
Sweet Afton, 23, 151
Szechuan Cucumber Salad, 184-86

tacos, 25, 72-73, 119, 133, 146, 173-74
  Barbacoa Lamb Tacos, 75-76
  Tacos al Suadero, 150
  Tacos la Familia, 173-74
  Tacos Morelos, 25
Tai Nam Gau Gan Sach, 149
tamales, 71-72, 155, 172, 174
  Tamales y Elote Cart, 172
Taramasalata (fish roe spread), 11
Taverna Kyclades, 5-10, 19, 24, 91
Tawa Food, 172
tawa kata-kat, 164
teas, tea, 24, 32, 67, 101
  bubble, 141, 151, 201
  butter, 166
  Chinese, 111, 191-94, 201
  insights on, 195
Tellez, Lesley, 75, 151
Telly's Taverna, 111-12
Terraza 7, 151
Thai food, 24-25, 166, 174-75, 203
  Drunken Noodles, 120-21
  in Elmhurst, 91, 98, 112, 138-39, 143-44, 149,
151
  in Jackson Heights, 119, 135
  Pad Kra Prao with Crispy Pork, 138
  Shredded Green Mango Salad, 122-24
  Shrimp with Thai Chile Sauce, 143-44
  in Woodside, 24, 117-24
Thai Grocery, 139, 149
Thailand's Center Point, 24, 175
Thenthuk, 166, 174
Tianjin Dumpling House, 111-12, 183-85, 200
Tibetan food, 89-90
  in Jackson Heights, 154-61, 165-70, 172, 174,
202

Phingsha (Beef Soup with Potatoes), 158, 166, 169-70
  Shabhaley (Tibetan-Style Empanadas), 167-68
  Shapta (Sautéed Sliced Beef), 157-59
  Sho-Go Khatsa (Aloo Dum), 158, 160-61
Tibet Mobile, 155, 172, 174, 202
Tipmanee, Lersak, 119-21, 123
Tipmanee, Sripraphai, 117, 119-20
Tirokafteri (Spicy Greek Cheese Dip), 18-19
Titan Foods, 4, 19, 60, 113
Tito Rad's Grill & Restaurant, 124-28
tlacoyos, 25
tlayudas, 88
tofu, 95, 106-7
  in Flushing, 184, 186, 195-96
tomatoes, tomato sauce, 3, 102, 105
  Greek Salad, 6-8, 81
  Lasagna, 71, 85-87
  Mexican-Style Seafood Cocktail, 145-48
  Okra and Tomato Mezze, 59-61
  Salsa Roja, 73-74
  Stuffed Cabbage with Tomato-Raisin Sauce, 49-51
Tony's Pizzeria & Restaurant, 71, 85-87
tortas, 70-71, 77-79, 133, 146
  Torta de Milanesa (Mexican-Style Breaded Chicken Cutlet), 78-79
Tortas Neza, 70-71, 77-79, 173-75, 202-3
tortillas, 71-73, 88
  Shrimp Enchiladas (Enchiladas Camerones), 76-77
Tortilleria Nixtamal, 71-77, 89, 91, 203
Tournesol, 31, 41
tourtiére (meat pie), 31
tuna, 125, 143

Uncle Zhou, 149
Upi Jaya, 139, 149
Urubamba, 25
Uruguayan food, 90-91, 172
U.S. Supermarket, 139, 142, 144-45

vegetables, 3, 19, 34-36, 125-26, 141-42, 144, 148, 156, 166, 169-71, 203
  Korean Barbecue Lettuce Wraps with Marinated Steak and Pickled Vegetables, 100-101

vegetarian food, 10, 36, 112
Vesta, 24-25
Via Trenta, 24
Vietnamese food:
  coffee and, 141, 145, 201
  in Elmhurst, 139-45, 149
  Lemongrass Chicken Banh Mi, 140-43

Wafa's, 58-62, 112, 203
Wang Wang Pot, 180
wheat:
  Cracked Wheat Pilaf (Pourgouri), 12-13, 100
  Mujadarah, 59-62
White Bear, 179, 200
wine, 16, 24, 195
  Red Wine Pork (Afelia) with Cracked Wheat Pilaf (Pourgouri), 12-13
Wong, Julie, 139-42, 144-45, 161
Wong, Scott, 139-42, 144-45
Wong, Theresa, 193-95
Woodside, 89-91, 114-35, 151, 202
  Asian food in, 24, 117-28, 132-33, 135
  bakeries in, 24, 91, 117-19
  butchers in, 114, 128-31
  desserts in, 91, 119, 125, 132
  Filipino food in, 119, 124-28, 132-33, 135
  food shops in, 114, 116, 119, 124, 128-33, 135
  Korean food in, 117
  Mexican food in, 119
  Thai food in, 24, 117-24

Xi'an Famous Foods, 65, 184, 202
Xinjiang BBQ Cart, 201

yak, 156-57, 166
yan balls, 196
Yi, Daniel, 95, 97-98, 100, 139
Young, Grace, 179

Zabb Elee, 203
Zeidaies, Freddy, 19-20
Zimmern, Andrew, 15, 164, 202
Zomsa, 166